FAVORITE BRAND NAME
ONION RECIPES

Publications International, Ltd.

Contents

Great Starters

Onion and Pepper Calzones

 1 teaspoon vegetable oil
½ cup chopped onion
½ cup chopped green bell pepper
¼ teaspoon salt
⅛ teaspoon dried basil leaves
⅛ teaspoon dried oregano leaves
⅛ teaspoon black pepper
 1 can (12 ounces) country biscuits
    (10 biscuits)
¼ cup (1 ounce) shredded mozzarella
    cheese
½ cup prepared spaghetti or pizza
    sauce
 2 tablespoons grated Parmesan
    cheese

1. Preheat oven to 400°F. Heat oil in medium nonstick skillet over medium-high heat. Add onion and bell pepper. Cook 5 minutes, stirring occasionally. Remove from heat. Add salt, basil, oregano and black pepper; stir to combine. Cool slightly.

2. While onion mixture is cooling, flatten biscuits into 3½-inch circles about ⅛ inch thick using palm of hand.

3. Stir mozzarella cheese into onion mixture; spoon 1 teaspoonful onto each biscuit. Fold biscuits in half, covering filling. Press edges with tines of fork to seal; transfer to baking sheet.

4. Bake 10 to 12 minutes or until golden brown. While calzones are baking, place spaghetti sauce in small microwavable bowl. Cover with vented plastic wrap. Microwave on HIGH 3 minutes or until hot.

5. To serve, spoon spaghetti sauce and Parmesan cheese evenly over each calzone. Serve immediately.

Makes 10 appetizers

Prep and Cook Time: 25 minutes

Green Onion Dip

 1 package (1 ounce) HIDDEN
    VALLEY® Milk Recipe Original
    Ranch® salad dressing mix
 1 cup mayonnaise
 1 cup (½ pint) sour cream
½ cup finely chopped green onions

In medium bowl, whisk together all ingredients. Refrigerate at least 1 hour before serving. Serve with fresh vegetables, such as cauliflowerets, carrot and celery sticks, cucumber slices, tomato wedges or turnip chips.

Makes about 2½ cups dip

Onion and Pepper Calzones

The Ultimate Onion

    3 cups cornstarch
1½ cups all-purpose flour
    2 teaspoons garlic salt
    2 teaspoons paprika
    1 teaspoon salt
    1 teaspoon black pepper
    2 bottles (24 ounces) beer
    4 to 6 Colossal onions (4 inches in
        diameter)
    2 cups all-purpose flour
    4 teaspoons paprika
    2 teaspoons garlic powder
 ½ teaspoon black pepper
 ¼ teaspoon cayenne pepper
    1 pint mayonnaise
    1 pint sour cream
 ½ cup chili sauce
 ½ teaspoon cayenne pepper

1. Mix cornstarch, 1½ cups flour, garlic salt, 2 teaspoons paprika, salt and 1 teaspoon black pepper in large bowl. Add beer; mix well. Set aside.

2. Cut about ¾-inch off top of each onion; peel. Being careful not to cut through bottom, cut each onion into 12 to 16 wedges.

3. Soak cut onions in ice water 10 to 15 minutes. If onions do not "bloom" cut petals slightly deeper. Meanwhile, prepare seasoned flour mixture; combine 2 cups flour, 4 teaspoons paprika, garlic powder, ½ teaspoon black pepper and ¼ teaspoon cayenne pepper in large bowl; mix well.

4. Dip cut onions into seasoned flour mixture; remove excess by shaking carefully. Dip in batter; remove excess by shaking carefully. Separate "petals" to coat thoroughly with batter. (If batter begins to separate, mix thoroughly before using.)

5. Gently place one onion in fryer basket and deep-fry at 375°F 1½ minutes. Turn onion over and fry 1 to 1½ minutes or until golden brown. Drain on paper towels. Place onion upright in shallow bowl and remove about 1 inch of "petals" from center of onion. Repeat with remaining onions.

6. Prepare creamy chili sauce; combine mayonnaise, sour cream, chili sauce and ½ teaspoon cayenne pepper in large bowl. Spoon chili sauce into small cups. Place one cup in center of each warm onion; serve.   *Makes 16 to 24 servings*

Favorite recipe from **National Onion Association**

Chili con Queso

    1 pound pasteurized process cheese
        spread, cut into cubes
    1 can (10 ounces) diced tomatoes
        and green chiles, undrained
    1 cup sliced green onions
    2 teaspoons ground coriander
    2 teaspoons ground cumin
 ¾ teaspoon hot pepper sauce
        Green onion strips (optional)
        Hot pepper slices (optional)

SLOW COOKER DIRECTIONS
Combine all ingredients *except* green onion strips and hot pepper slices in slow cooker until well blended. Cover and cook on LOW 2 to 3 hours or until hot. Garnish with green onion strips and hot pepper slices, if desired.   *Makes 3 cups dip*

The Ultimate Onion

Savory Herb-Stuffed Onions

1 zucchini, cut lengthwise into
    ¼-inch-thick slices
3 shiitake mushrooms
4 large sweet onions
1 plum tomato, seeded and chopped
2 tablespoons fresh bread crumbs
1 tablespoon fresh basil *or*
    1 teaspoon dried basil
1 teaspoon olive oil
¼ teaspoon salt
⅛ teaspoon ground black pepper
4 teaspoons balsamic vinegar

1. Grill zucchini on uncovered grill over medium coals 4 minutes or until tender, turning once. Cool; cut into bite-sized pieces.

2. Thread mushrooms onto metal skewers. Grill on covered grill over medium coals 20 to 30 minutes or until tender. Coarsely chop; set aside.

3. Remove stem and root ends of onions, leaving peels intact. Spray onions with nonstick cooking spray; grill root-end up on covered grill over medium coals 5 minutes or until lightly charred. Remove and let stand until cool enough to handle. Peel and scoop about 1 inch of pulp from stem ends; chop for filling and set whole onions aside.

4. Combine chopped onion, mushrooms, zucchini, tomato, bread crumbs, basil, oil, salt and pepper in large bowl; mix until well blended. Spoon stuffing mixture evenly into center of each onion.

5. Place each onion on sheet of foil; sprinkle each with 1 tablespoon water. Seal; grill onion packets on covered grill over medium coals 45 to 60 minutes or until tender. Spoon 1 teaspoon vinegar over each onion before serving.

Makes 4 appetizer servings

Beef Appetizer Kabobs

1 (7-ounce) jar roasted red peppers,
    drained, finely chopped
½ cup A.1.® Original or A.1.® Bold &
    Spicy Steak Sauce
⅓ cup ketchup
¼ cup chopped fresh parsley
2 teaspoons dried oregano leaves
1 (1½-pound) beef top round steak,
    cut into ¾-inch cubes (about
    72 cubes)
16 green onions, cut into 1-inch pieces
24 fresh mushroom caps

Soak 24 (10-inch) wooden skewers in water at least 30 minutes.

In small bowl, blend peppers, steak sauce, ketchup, parsley and oregano; reserve ½ cup for basting kabobs. Set aside remaining pepper mixture for serving with kabobs.

Alternately thread 3 steak cubes, 2 green onion pieces and 1 mushroom cap onto each skewer. Grill kabobs over medium heat or broil 6 inches from heat source 10 to 15 minutes or until steak is of desired doneness, turning and basting often with ½ cup basting sauce. Serve with remaining pepper mixture.

Makes 24 appetizers

Savory Herb-Stuffed Onions

Meat-Filled Samosas

1 cup all-purpose flour
1 cup whole-wheat flour
1¼ teaspoons salt, divided
2 tablespoons plus 2 teaspoons vegetable oil, divided
⅓ to ½ cup water
1 small onion, finely chopped
2 cloves garlic, minced
1 teaspoon finely chopped fresh ginger
¾ pound lean ground lamb or ground round
2 teaspoons Garam Masala* (recipe follows)
¾ cup frozen peas
1 small tomato, peeled, seeded and chopped
2 teaspoons finely chopped cilantro
1 jalapeño pepper,** seeded and chopped
Additional vegetable oil for frying
Cilantro Chutney (recipe follows) (optional)

Also available at specialty stores and Indian markets.

**Jalapeño peppers can sting and irritate the skin; wear rubber gloves when handling peppers and do not touch eyes. Wash hands after handling.*

Combine flours and ½ teaspoon salt in large bowl. Stir in 2 tablespoons oil with fork; mix until mixture resembles fine crumbs. Gradually stir in enough water, about ⅓ cup, until dough forms a ball and is no longer sticky. Place dough on lightly floured surface; flatten slightly. Knead dough 5 minutes or until smooth and elastic. Divide dough in half and form 2 ropes, each about 9 inches long and 1 inch thick. Wrap in plastic wrap; let stand 1 hour.

Meanwhile, heat remaining 2 teaspoons oil in large skillet over medium heat. Add onion, garlic and ginger; cook and stir 5 minutes or until onion is softened.

Crumble meat into skillet; cook 6 to 8 minutes or until browned, stirring to separate meat. Spoon off and discard fat. Stir in Garam Masala and remaining ¾ teaspoon salt. Add peas, tomato, cilantro and jalapeño to skillet; mix well. Cover and cook 5 minutes or until peas are heated through. Cool to room temperature before filling samosas.

To form samosas, divide each rope of dough into 9 equal portions. Roll each piece on lightly floured surface into 4- to 5-inch round. Keep remaining dough pieces wrapped in plastic wrap to prevent drying. Cut each round of dough in half, forming 2 semi-circles. Moisten straight edge of 1 semi-circle with water and fold in half; press moistened edges together to seal. Spread dough apart to form cone; fill with 2 teaspoons meat filling. Press meat mixture into cone, leaving ½ inch of dough above meat mixture. Moisten edges of dough and press firmly together. Place samosas on work surface and seal edges with fork.

Heat 3 to 4 inches oil in large heavy skillet over medium-high heat to 375°F on deep-fat thermometer. Cook 4 to 6 samosas at a time 3 to 4 minutes or until crisp and golden. Drain on paper towels. Serve with Cilantro Chutney, if desired.

Makes 36 samosas

Garam Masala

2 teaspoons cumin seeds
2 teaspoons whole black peppercorns
1½ teaspoons coriander seeds
1 teaspoon fennel seeds
¾ teaspoon whole cloves
½ teaspoon whole cardamom seeds, pods removed
1 cinnamon stick, broken

Preheat oven to 250°F. Combine spices in baking pan; bake 30 minutes, stirring occasionally. Transfer spices to clean coffee or spice grinder or use mortar and pestle to pulverize. Store in covered glass jar.

Cilantro Chutney

½ cup green onions, cut into ½-inch
   lengths
1 to 2 hot green chili peppers,
   seeded and coarsely chopped
2 tablespoons chopped fresh ginger
2 cloves garlic, peeled
1 cup packed cilantro leaves
2 tablespoons vegetable oil
2 tablespoons lime juice
1 teaspoon salt
1 teaspoon sugar
¼ teaspoon ground cumin

Drop green onions, chilies, ginger and garlic through feed tube of food processor with motor running. Stop machine and add cilantro, oil, lime juice, salt, sugar and cumin; process until cilantro is finely chopped.

CHOPPING ONIONS

1. Peel skin from onion; cut in half through the root.

2. Make cuts parallel to cutting board, almost to root end.

3. Make vertical, lengthwise cuts. Slice across cuts to root end.

Onion and Pepper Quesadillas

1 tablespoon olive or salad oil
2 medium green bell peppers,
   seeded and thinly sliced
1 medium onion, thinly sliced
2 teaspoons chili powder
1 teaspoon ground cumin
1 clove garlic, minced
¼ teaspoon cayenne pepper
½ cup pitted California ripe olives,
   coarsely chopped
6 flour tortillas (7 to 9 inches)
¾ cup shredded Cheddar cheese
¾ cup shredded Monterey Jack
   cheese
Reduced-fat sour cream

Heat large skillet over medium-high heat. Add oil, bell peppers, onion, chili powder, cumin, garlic and cayenne, stirring often, until peppers and onion are soft, about 5 minutes. Remove pan from heat and stir in chopped olives; set aside. Arrange 3 tortillas in single layer on 2 baking sheets. Divide bell pepper mixture evenly among tortillas; spread to ½ inch of edges. Evenly cover with cheeses, then top each tortilla with one of remaining tortillas; press lightly. Bake at 450°F until tortillas are lightly browned, 7 to 9 minutes, switching positions of baking sheets halfway through baking. Cut each into 4 or 6 wedges. Arrange on platter and add sour cream to taste. Garnish with sliced olives.

Makes 6 servings

Prep Time: 15 minutes
Cook Time: 12 to 14 minutes

Favorite recipe from **California Olive Industry**

Stuffed Pesto Torta

2 tablespoons olive oil
1 cup chopped onion
3 cloves garlic, minced
1 can (14½ ounces) Italian-style
 tomatoes, undrained and
 chopped
2 tablespoons tomato paste
2 teaspoons dry Italian seasoning
½ teaspoon salt
½ teaspoon crushed red pepper
 flakes
1 package (3 ounces) cream cheese,
 softened
½ cup (2 ounces) freshly grated
 Parmesan cheese
⅓ cup whole-milk ricotta cheese
¼ teaspoon black pepper
1 pound fresh uncooked Italian
 sausage, casings removed
1 package (17¼ ounces) frozen puff
 pastry, thawed
½ pound thinly sliced Gruyère or
 mozzarella cheese
6 tablespoons pesto
1 egg yolk
1 teaspoon water

Heat oil in medium saucepan over medium-high heat until hot; add onion and garlic. Cook 2 minutes or until onion is tender. Add tomatoes with liquid, tomato paste, Italian seasoning, salt and red pepper; bring to a boil. Reduce heat to low; simmer, uncovered, 30 minutes or until mixture reduces to 1⅓ cups. Remove from heat; set aside.

Meanwhile, combine cream cheese, Parmesan and ricotta cheeses and black pepper in medium bowl; beat with electric mixer at medium speed until smooth. Set aside.

Brown sausage in large skillet over medium-high heat until no longer pink, stirring to separate meat. Drain sausage on paper towels; set aside.

Preheat oven to 375°F. Roll out 1 pastry sheet to 13-inch square on lightly floured surface with lightly floured rolling pin. Press pastry onto bottom and up side of 9-inch springform pan. (Pastry will not completely cover side of pan and will hang over edge in places.)

Layer ½ of cooked sausage on bottom of pastry shell. Top with ½ of reserved tomato sauce mixture, spreading evenly. Drop ½ of cream cheese mixture by heaping teaspoonfuls over tomato sauce mixture. Arrange ½ of Gruyère in pastry shell, forming solid layer. Spread pesto evenly over Gruyère with small metal spatula. Arrange remaining Gruyère over pesto, forming another solid layer. Drop remaining cream cheese mixture by heaping teaspoonfuls over Gruyère. Top with remaining tomato sauce mixture. Layer with remaining cooked sausage. Trim overhanging pastry to an even height with paring knife. Fold pastry over filling.

Roll out remaining pastry sheet to 12-inch square on lightly floured surface; trim to 8-inch circle. Make decorative pastry cut-outs from excess dough, if desired. Beat egg yolk and water in small bowl; lightly brush on pastry around filled torta. Carefully place 8-inch circle of pastry over torta, pressing gently to adhere. Lightly brush top crust with egg mixture and arrange pastry cut-outs on top. Brush cut-outs with egg mixture.

Bake 1 hour or until pastry is golden. Let stand 15 minutes on wire rack. To serve, carefully remove side of pan; let stand 45 minutes before cutting into wedges. Garnish as desired.

Makes 24 appetizer servings

Stuffed Pesto Torta

Cheese and Pepper Stuffed Potato Skins

6 large russet potatoes (about
    ¾ pound each), scrubbed
4 tablespoons FRANK'S® REDHOT®
    Hot Sauce, divided
2 tablespoons butter, melted
1 large red bell pepper, seeded and
    finely chopped
1 cup chopped green onions
1 cup (4 ounces) shredded Cheddar
    cheese

1. Preheat oven to 450°F. Wrap potatoes in foil; bake about 1 hour 15 minutes or until fork tender. Let stand until cool enough to handle. Cut each potato in half lengthwise; scoop out insides*, leaving a ¼-inch-thick shell. Cut shells in half crosswise. Place shells on large baking sheet.

2. Preheat broiler. Combine 1 tablespoon REDHOT sauce and butter in small bowl; brush on inside of each potato shell. Broil shells, 6 inches from heat, 8 minutes or until golden brown and crispy.

3. Combine remaining 3 tablespoons REDHOT sauce with remaining ingredients in large bowl. Spoon about 1 tablespoon mixture into each potato shell. Broil 2 minutes or until cheese melts. Cut each piece in half to serve.

Makes 12 servings

Reserve leftover potato for mashed potatoes, home-fries or soup.

Prep Time: 30 minutes

Cook Time: 1 hour 25 minutes

Savory Corn Cakes

2 cups all-purpose flour
1 teaspoon baking powder
½ teaspoon salt
2 cups frozen corn, thawed
1 cup fat-free (skim) milk
1 cup (4 ounces) shredded smoked
    Cheddar cheese
2 egg whites, beaten
1 whole egg, beaten
4 green onions, finely chopped
2 cloves garlic, minced
1 tablespoon chili powder
    Prepared salsa (optional)

1. Combine flour, baking powder and salt in large bowl with wire whisk. Stir in corn, milk, cheese, egg whites, egg, green onions, garlic and chili powder until well blended.

2. Spray large nonstick skillet with nonstick cooking spray; heat over medium-high heat.

3. Drop batter by ¼ cupfuls into skillet. Cook 3 minutes per side or until golden brown. Serve with prepared salsa.

Makes 12 cakes

*Cheese and Pepper Stuffed
Potato Skins*

Come for Brunch

Scrambled Eggs with Tomatoes & Chilies

  8 eggs
  ½ teaspoon salt
  2 tablespoons butter or margarine
  2 tablespoons vegetable oil
  ⅓ cup finely chopped white onion
  2 to 4 fresh serrano chilies, finely
      chopped*
  2 medium tomatoes, seeded,
      chopped, drained
  Cilantro sprigs for garnish
  Warm corn tortillas (optional)
  Fresh fruit (optional)

Jalapeño peppers can sting and irritate the skin; wear rubber gloves when handling peppers and do not touch eyes. Wash hands after handling.

1. Whisk eggs and salt lightly in medium bowl.

2. Heat butter and oil in large skillet over medium heat until hot. Add onion and chilies. Cook and stir 45 seconds or until hot but not soft.

3. Stir in tomatoes. Increase heat to medium-high. Cook and stir 45 seconds or until tomatoes are very hot.

4. Add egg mixture all at once to skillet. Cook without stirring 1 minute. Cook 2 to 3 minutes more, stirring lightly until eggs are softly set. Garnish, if desired. Serve with tortillas and fruit.

Makes 4 servings

Note: Fresh chilies provide crunchy texture that cannot be duplicated with canned chilies. For milder flavor, seed some or all of the chilies.

Potato & Onion Frittata

  1 small baking potato, peeled, halved
      and sliced ⅛-inch thick (about
      ½ cup)
  ¼ cup chopped onion
  1 clove garlic, minced
      Dash ground black pepper
  1 tablespoon FLEISCHMANN'S®
      Original Margarine
  1 cup EGG BEATERS® Healthy Real
      Egg Product

In 8-inch nonstick skillet, over medium-high heat, sauté potato, onion, garlic and pepper in margarine until tender. Pour Egg Beaters evenly into skillet over potato mixture. Cook without stirring for 5 to 6 minutes or until cooked on bottom and almost set on top. Carefully turn frittata; cook for 1 to 2 minutes more or until done. Slide onto serving platter; cut into wedges to serve.   *Makes 2 servings*

Prep Time: 5 minutes
Cook Time: 15 minutes

*Scrambled Eggs with
Tomatoes & Chilies*

Onion-Zucchini Bread

1 large zucchini (¾ pound), shredded
2½ cups all-purpose flour*
⅓ cup grated Parmesan cheese
1⅓ cups FRENCH'S® French Fried Onions
1 tablespoon baking powder
1 tablespoon chopped fresh basil or 1 teaspoon dried basil leaves
½ teaspoon salt
¾ cup milk
½ cup (1 stick) butter or margarine, melted
¼ cup packed light brown sugar
2 eggs

*You may substitute 1¼ cups whole-wheat flour for 1¼ cups of all-purpose flour.

Preheat oven to 350°F. Grease 9×5×3-inch loaf pan.

Drain zucchini in colander. Combine flour, cheese, French Fried Onions, baking powder, basil and salt in large bowl.

Combine milk, butter, brown sugar and eggs in medium bowl; whisk until well blended. Place zucchini in kitchen towel; squeeze out excess liquid. Stir zucchini into milk mixture.

Stir milk mixture into flour mixture, stirring just until moistened. Do not overmix. (Batter will be very stiff and dry.) Spoon batter into prepared pan. Run knife down center of batter.

Bake 50 to 65 minutes or until toothpick inserted in center comes out clean. Cool in pan on wire rack 10 minutes. Remove bread from pan to wire rack; cool completely. Cut into slices to serve.**

Makes 10 to 12 servings

**For optimum flavor, wrap bread overnight and serve the next day. Great when toasted!

Prep Time: 20 minutes

Cook Time: about 1 hour

Double Onion Quiche

3 cups thinly sliced yellow onions
3 tablespoons butter or margarine
1 cup thinly sliced green onions
3 eggs
1 cup heavy cream
½ cup grated Parmesan cheese
¼ teaspoon hot pepper sauce
1 package (1 ounce) HIDDEN VALLEY® Milk Recipe Original Ranch® salad dressing mix
1 (9-inch) deep-dish pastry shell, baked, cooled
Fresh oregano sprig for garnish

Preheat oven to 350°F. In medium skillet, cook and stir yellow onions in butter, stirring occasionally, about 10 minutes. Add green onions; cook 5 minutes. Remove from heat; cool.

In large bowl, whisk eggs until frothy. Whisk in cream, cheese, pepper sauce and salad dressing mix. Stir in cooled onion mixture. Pour egg and onion mixture into cooled pastry shell. Bake until top is browned and knife inserted in center comes out clean, 35 to 40 minutes. Cool on wire rack 10 minutes before slicing. Garnish with oregano.

Makes 8 servings

Onion-Zucchini Bread

Onion, Cheese and Tomato Tart

Parmesan-Pepper Dough (recipe follows)
1 tablespoon butter
1 medium onion, thinly sliced
1 cup (4 ounces) shredded Swiss cheese
2 to 3 ripe tomatoes, sliced
Black pepper
2 tablespoons snipped fresh chives

1. Prepare Parmesan-Pepper Dough.

2. Melt butter in large skillet over medium heat. Add onion; cook and stir 20 minutes or until tender.

3. Spread onion over prepared dough. Sprinkle with cheese. Let rise in warm place 20 to 30 minutes or until edges are puffy.

4. Preheat oven to 400°F. Top dough with tomatoes. Sprinkle with pepper. Bake 25 minutes or until edges are deep golden and cheese is melted. Let cool 10 minutes. Transfer to serving platter. Sprinkle with chives. Cut into wedges.

Makes 6 to 8 servings

Parmesan-Pepper Dough

1 package (¼ ounce) active dry yeast
1 tablespoon sugar
⅔ cup warm water (105° to 115°F)
2 cups all-purpose flour, divided
¼ cup grated Parmesan cheese
1 teaspoon salt
½ teaspoon black pepper
1 tablespoon olive oil

1. Sprinkle yeast and sugar over warm water in small bowl; stir until yeast is dissolved. Let stand 5 minutes or until mixture is bubbly.

2. Combine 1¾ cups flour, cheese, salt and pepper in large bowl. Pour yeast mixture and oil over flour mixture and stir until mixture clings together.

3. Turn out dough onto lightly floured surface. Knead 8 to 10 minutes or until smooth and elastic, adding remaining ¼ cup flour if necessary. Shape dough into a ball; place in large greased bowl. Turn dough so that top is greased. Cover with towel; let rise in warm place 1 hour or until doubled in bulk.

4. Punch down dough. Knead on lightly floured surface 1 minute or until smooth. Flatten into a disc. Roll dough to make 11-inch round. Press into bottom and up side of buttered 9- or 10-inch tart pan with removable bottom.

Spicy Onion Bread

2 tablespoons instant minced onion
⅓ cup water
1½ cups biscuit mix
1 egg, slightly beaten
½ cup milk
½ teaspoon TABASCO® brand Pepper Sauce
2 tablespoons butter, melted
½ teaspoon caraway seeds (optional)

Preheat oven to 400°F. Soak instant minced onion in water 5 minutes. Combine biscuit mix, egg, milk and TABASCO® Sauce in large bowl and stir until blended. Stir in onion. Turn into greased 8-inch pie plate. Brush with melted butter. Sprinkle with caraway seeds. Bake 20 to 25 minutes or until golden brown. *Makes 8 servings*

Onion, Cheese and Tomato Tart

Feta Brunch Bake

1 medium red bell pepper
2 bags (10 ounces *each*) fresh
    spinach, washed and stemmed
6 eggs
6 ounces crumbled feta cheese
⅓ cup chopped onion
2 tablespoons chopped fresh parsley
¼ teaspoon dried dill weed
    Dash ground black pepper

Preheat broiler. Place bell pepper on foil-lined broiler pan. Broil, 4 inches from heat, 15 to 20 minutes or until blackened on all sides, turning every 5 minutes with tongs. Place in paper bag; close bag and set aside to cool about 15 to 20 minutes. To peel pepper, cut around core, twist and remove. Cut in half and peel off skin with paring knife; rinse under cold water to remove seeds. Cut into ½-inch pieces.

Blanch spinach; squeeze to remove excess water. Finely chop spinach.

Preheat oven to 400°F. Grease 1-quart baking dish. Beat eggs in large bowl with electric mixer at medium speed until foamy. Stir in bell pepper, spinach, cheese, onion, parsley, dill weed and black pepper. Pour egg mixture into prepared dish. Bake 20 minutes or until set. Let stand 5 minutes before serving. Garnish as desired.

Makes 4 servings

Crispy Onion Crescent Rolls

1 can (8 ounces) refrigerated
    crescent dinner rolls
1⅓ cups FRENCH'S® French Fried
    Onions, slightly crushed
1 egg, beaten

Preheat oven to 375°F. Line large baking sheet with foil. Separate refrigerated rolls into 8 triangles. Sprinkle center of each triangle with about *1½ tablespoons* French Fried Onions. Roll-up triangles from short side, jelly-roll fashion. Sprinkle any excess onions over top of crescents.

Arrange crescents on prepared baking sheet. Brush with beaten egg. Bake 15 minutes or until golden brown and crispy. Transfer to wire rack; cool slightly.

Makes 8 servings

Prep Time: 15 minutes
Cook Time: 15 minutes

ONION TIP

Eat leeks in March and ramsins in May, and all the year after the physicians may play.
-Old English proverb

Feta Brunch Bake

Spicy Mexican Frittata

1 fresh jalapeño pepper*
1 clove garlic
1 medium tomato, peeled, halved, seeded and quartered
½ teaspoon ground coriander
½ teaspoon chili powder
½ cup chopped onion
1 cup frozen corn
6 egg whites
2 eggs
¼ cup fat-free (skim) milk
¼ teaspoon salt
¼ teaspoon black pepper
¼ cup (1 ounce) shredded part-skim farmer or mozzarella cheese

*Jalapeño peppers can sting and irritate the skin; wear rubber gloves when handling peppers and do not touch eyes. Wash hands after handling.

Add jalapeño pepper and garlic to food processor or blender; process until finely chopped. Add tomato, coriander and chili powder. Cover; process until tomato is almost smooth.

Spray large skillet with nonstick cooking spray; heat over medium heat. Add onion to skillet; cook and stir until tender. Stir in tomato mixture and corn. Cook 3 to 4 minutes or until liquid is almost evaporated, stirring occasionally.

Combine egg whites, eggs, milk, salt and black pepper in medium bowl. Add egg mixture all at once to skillet. Cook, without stirring, 2 minutes until eggs begin to set. Run large spoon around edge of skillet, lifting eggs for even cooking. Remove skillet from heat when eggs are almost set but surface is still moist.

Sprinkle with cheese. Cover; let stand 3 to 4 minutes or until surface is set and cheese melts. Cut into wedges.

Makes 4 servings

Mushroom & Onion Egg Bake

1 tablespoon vegetable oil
4 green onions, chopped
4 ounces mushrooms, sliced
1 cup low-fat cottage cheese
1 cup sour cream
6 eggs
2 tablespoons all-purpose flour
¼ teaspoon salt
⅛ teaspoon freshly ground pepper
Dash hot pepper sauce

1. Preheat oven to 350°F. Grease shallow 1-quart baking dish.

2. Heat oil in medium skillet over medium heat. Add onions and mushrooms; cook until tender. Set aside.

3. Place cottage cheese in blender or food processor, process until almost smooth. Add sour cream, eggs, flour, salt, pepper and hot pepper sauce; process until combined. Stir in onions and mushrooms. Pour into prepared dish. Bake about 40 minutes or until knife inserted near center comes out clean.

Makes about 6 servings

Spicy Mexican Frittata

The Pasta Bowl

Creamy "Crab" Fettuccine

6 ounces uncooked fettuccine
3 tablespoons margarine or butter,
    divided
1 small onion, chopped
2 ribs celery, chopped
½ medium red bell pepper, chopped
2 cloves garlic, minced
1 cup reduced-fat sour cream
1 cup reduced-fat mayonnaise
1 cup (4 ounces) shredded sharp
    Cheddar cheese
2 tablespoons chopped fresh parsley
¼ teaspoon salt
⅛ teaspoon black pepper
1 pound imitation crabmeat sticks,
    cut into bite-size pieces
½ cup cornflake crumbs
    Fresh chives (optional)

Preheat oven to 350°F. Spray 2-quart square baking dish with nonstick cooking spray. Cook pasta according to package directions. Drain and set aside.

Meanwhile, melt 1 tablespoon margarine in large skillet over medium-high heat. Add onion, celery, bell pepper and garlic; cook and stir 2 minutes or until vegetables are tender.

Combine sour cream, mayonnaise, cheese, parsley, salt and black pepper in large bowl. Add crabmeat, pasta and vegetable mixture, stirring gently to combine. Pour into prepared dish.

Melt remaining 2 tablespoons margarine. Combine cornflake crumbs and margarine in small bowl; sprinkle over casserole.

Bake, uncovered, 30 minutes or until hot. Garnish if desired.   *Makes 6 servings*

Baked Ziti with Walnuts

1 cup uncooked ziti pasta
1 box (10 ounces) BIRDS EYE® frozen
    Peas & Pearl Onions
1 cup tomato sauce
½ cup chopped walnuts
1 tablespoon olive oil
2 tablespoons grated Parmesan
    cheese

• Preheat oven to 350°F.

• Cook ziti according to package directions; drain and set aside.

• In large bowl, combine vegetables, tomato sauce, walnuts and oil. Add ziti; toss well.

• Place mixture in 13×9-inch baking pan. Sprinkle with cheese.

• Bake 20 minutes or until heated through.   *Makes 4 servings*

Prep Time: 10 minutes

Cook Time: 20 minutes

Creamy "Crab" Fettuccine

Pasta with Onions and Goat Cheese

2 teaspoons olive oil
4 cups thinly sliced sweet onions
¾ cup (3 ounces) goat cheese
¼ cup fat-free (skim) milk
6 ounces uncooked baby bow tie or other small pasta
1 clove garlic, minced
2 tablespoons dry white wine or fat-free reduced-sodium chicken broth
1½ teaspoons chopped fresh sage *or* ½ teaspoon dried sage leaves
½ teaspoon salt
¼ teaspoon black pepper
2 tablespoons chopped toasted walnuts

Heat oil in large nonstick skillet over medium heat. Add onions; cook slowly until golden and caramelized, about 20 to 25 minutes, stirring occasionally.

Combine goat cheese and milk in small bowl; stir until well blended. Set aside.

Cook pasta according to package directions, omitting salt. Drain and set aside.

Add garlic to onions in skillet; cook until softened, about 3 minutes. Add wine, sage, salt and pepper; cook until moisture is evaporated. Remove from heat; add pasta and goat cheese mixture, stirring to melt cheese. Sprinkle with walnuts.

Makes 8 (½-cup) servings

Cheeseburger Macaroni

1 cup mostaccioli or elbow macaroni, uncooked
1 pound ground beef
1 medium onion, chopped
1 can (14½ ounces) DEL MONTE® Diced Tomatoes with Basil, Garlic & Oregano
¼ cup DEL MONTE® Tomato Ketchup
1 cup (4 ounces) shredded Cheddar cheese

1. Cook pasta according to package directions; drain.

2. Brown beef with onion in large skillet; drain. Season with salt and pepper, if desired. Stir in tomatoes, ketchup and pasta; heat through.

3. Top with cheese. Garnish, if desired.

Makes 4 servings

Prep Time: 8 minutes

Cook Time: 15 minutes

ONION TIP
Does chopping onions make you cry? Sometimes chilling the onions before cutting can help reduce the tearing effects.

Pasta with Onions and Goat Cheese

Beef Stroganoff Casserole

1 pound lean ground beef
¼ teaspoon salt
⅛ teaspoon black pepper
1 teaspoon vegetable oil
8 ounces sliced mushrooms
1 large onion, chopped
3 cloves garlic, minced
¼ cup dry white wine
1 can (10¾ ounces) condensed
   cream of mushroom soup,
   undiluted
½ cup sour cream
1 tablespoon Dijon mustard
4 cups cooked egg noodles
   Chopped fresh parsley (optional)

Preheat oven to 350°F. Spray 13×9-inch baking dish with nonstick cooking spray.

Place beef in large skillet; season with salt and pepper. Brown beef over medium-high heat until no longer pink, stirring to separate beef. Drain fat from skillet; set beef aside.

Heat oil in same skillet over medium-high heat until hot. Add mushrooms, onion and garlic; cook and stir 2 minutes or until onion is tender. Add wine. Reduce heat to medium-low and simmer 3 minutes. Remove from heat; stir in soup, sour cream and mustard until well combined. Return beef to skillet.

Place noodles in prepared dish. Pour beef mixture over noodles; stir until noodles are well coated.

Bake, uncovered, 30 minutes or until heated through. Sprinkle with parsley, if desired. *Makes 6 servings*

Pasta with Spinach-Cheese Sauce

¼ cup FILIPPO BERIO® Extra-Virgin
   Olive Oil, divided
1 medium onion, chopped
1 clove garlic, chopped
3 cups chopped fresh spinach,
   washed and well drained
1 cup low-fat ricotta or cottage
   cheese
½ cup chopped fresh parsley
1 teaspoon dried basil leaves
1 teaspoon lemon juice
¼ teaspoon black pepper
¼ teaspoon ground nutmeg
¾ pound uncooked spaghetti

1. Heat 3 tablespoons olive oil in large skillet over medium heat. Cook and stir onion and garlic until onion is tender.

2. Add spinach to skillet; cook 3 to 5 minutes or until spinach wilts.

3. Place spinach mixture, cheese, parsley, basil, lemon juice, pepper and nutmeg in covered blender container. Blend until smooth. Leave in blender, covered, to keep sauce warm.

4. Cook pasta according to package directions. Do not overcook. Drain pasta, reserving ¼ cup water. In large bowl, toss pasta with remaining 1 tablespoon olive oil.

5. Add reserved ¼ cup water to sauce in blender. Blend; serve over pasta.
Makes 4 servings

Beef Stroganoff Casserole

Paprika Pork with Spinach

1 pound boneless pork loin or leg
3 tablespoons all-purpose flour
3 tablespoons vegetable oil
1 cup frozen pearl onions, thawed
1 tablespoon paprika
1 can (14½ ounces) vegetable or chicken broth
8 ounces medium curly egg noodles, uncooked
1 package (10 ounces) frozen leaf spinach, thawed and well drained
½ cup sour cream

• Trim fat from pork; discard. Cut pork into 1-inch cubes. Place flour and pork in resealable plastic food storage bag; shake until well coated.

• Heat wok over high heat about 1 minute or until hot. Drizzle oil into wok and heat 30 seconds. Add pork; stir-fry about 5 minutes or until well browned on all sides. Remove pork to large bowl.

• Add onions and paprika to wok; stir-fry 1 minute. Stir in broth, noodles and pork. Cover and bring to a boil. Reduce heat to low; cook about 8 minutes or until noodles and pork are tender, stirring occasionally.

• Stir spinach into pork and noodles. Cover and cook until heated through. Add additional water if needed. Add sour cream; mix well. Transfer to serving dish. Garnish, if desired. *Makes 4 servings*

Pasta Peperonata

Olive oil-flavored cooking spray
4 cups sliced green, red and yellow bell peppers (about 1 large pepper of *each* color)
4 cups sliced onions
3 cloves garlic, minced
1 teaspoon dried basil leaves
½ teaspoon dried marjoram leaves
Salt and black pepper
4 ounces spaghetti or linguini, cooked and kept warm
4 teaspoons grated Parmesan cheese

1. Spray large skillet with cooking spray. Heat over medium heat until hot. Add bell peppers, onions, garlic, basil and marjoram; cook, covered, 8 to 10 minutes or until vegetables are wilted. Uncover; cook and stir 20 to 30 minutes or until onions are caramelized and mixture is soft and creamy. Season to taste with salt and black pepper.

2. Spoon pasta onto plates; top with peperonata and cheese.

Makes 6 side-dish servings

ONION TIP
During the Middle Ages, onions were so valuable, they were used as rent payments and as wedding gifts.

Pasta Peperonata

Beef & Pork

Blue Cheese Burgers with Red Onion

2 pounds ground chuck
2 cloves garlic, minced
1 teaspoon salt
½ teaspoon black pepper
4 ounces blue cheese
⅓ cup coarsely chopped walnuts, toasted
1 torpedo (long) red onion *or* 2 small red onions, sliced into ⅜-inch-thick rounds
2 baguettes (each 12 inches long)
Olive or vegetable oil

Combine beef, garlic, salt and pepper in medium bowl. Shape meat mixture into 12 oval patties. Mash cheese and blend with walnuts in small bowl. Divide cheese mixture equally; place onto centers of 6 meat patties. Top with remaining meat patties; tightly pinch edges together to seal in filling.

Oil hot grid to help prevent sticking. Grill patties and onion, if desired, on covered grill, over medium **KINGSFORD®** Briquets, 7 to 12 minutes for medium doneness, turning once. Cut baguettes into 4-inch lengths; split each piece and brush cut side with olive oil. Move cooked burgers to edge of grill to keep warm. Grill bread, oil side down, until lightly toasted. Serve burgers on toasted baguettes.

Makes 6 servings

Zesty Onion Meat Loaf

1½ pounds ground beef
1 can (10¾ ounces) condensed Italian tomato soup, divided
1⅓ cups FRENCH'S® French Fried Onions, divided
2 tablespoons FRENCH'S® Worcestershire Sauce
¾ teaspoon salt
¼ teaspoon ground pepper
1 egg

Preheat oven to 350°F. Combine beef, ⅓ cup soup, ⅔ *cup* French Fried Onions, Worcestershire, salt, pepper and egg in large bowl. Shape into 8×4-inch loaf. Place in shallow baking pan.

Bake 1 hour or until meat loaf is no longer pink in center and meat thermometer inserted in center registers 160°F. Pour off drippings; discard.

Spoon remaining soup over meat loaf. Top with remaining ⅔ *cup* onions. Bake 5 minutes or until onions are golden.

Makes 6 servings

Prep Time: 10 minutes
Cook Time: about 1 hour

Blue Cheese Burger with Red Onion

Red Cloud Beef and Onions

2¼ cups nonfat milk
1½ cups water
1½ cups yellow cornmeal
½ cup grated Parmesan cheese
1 tablespoon butter or margarine
4 medium yellow onions, sliced
　　(1 pound 6 ounces)
2 teaspoons vegetable oil
1 pound lean ground beef or pork
2 to 3 teaspoons chili powder
　　(to taste)
½ cup canned whole pimientos or
　　roasted red bell peppers, cut into
　　½-inch strips
2 cans (4 ounces *each)* whole green
　　chilies, cut into ½-inch strips
　　Sour cream (optional)

For cornmeal base, combine milk, water and cornmeal in saucepan. Place over medium heat and cook, stirring, until mixture bubbles. Continue cooking 30 to 60 seconds or until mixture is consistency of soft mashed potatoes. Remove from heat; stir in cheese and butter. Spoon into 2½-quart casserole. Sauté onions in oil in large skillet until soft and tender. Spoon into casserole in ring around edge. In same skillet, sauté beef until browned; stir in chili powder. Spoon into center of casserole. Arrange pimientos and chilies in latticework pattern over top. Cover and bake at 400°F for 25 to 30 minutes or until hot in center. Serve with dollops of sour cream, if desired.　　*Makes 6 servings*

Favorite recipe from **National Onion Association**

Pork and Pasta Skillet Supper

1 pound ground pork
1 medium onion, chopped
1 can (14½ ounces) pasta-ready
　　tomatoes
1 can (8 ounces) tomato sauce
1 small yellow summer squash or
　　zucchini, thinly sliced
1½ cups (4 ounces uncooked) hot
　　cooked penne pasta, or other
　　small shape pasta

1. Heat nonstick skillet over medium-high heat. Add pork and onion; cook and stir until evenly browned.

2. Stir in tomatoes and tomato sauce; bring to a boil. Reduce heat to low; cook 5 minutes.

3. Stir in squash and pasta. Cook 2 to 5 minutes or until heated through.
　　Makes 4 servings

Note: Serve with a crisp green salad and French bread.

Prep Time: 15 minutes

Favorite recipe from **National Pork Producers Council**

Red Cloud Beef and Onions

Kublai Khan's Stir-Fry with Fiery Walnuts

Fiery Walnuts (recipe follows)
1 pound boneless tender beef steak (sirloin, rib eye or top loin) or lamb sirloin
2 tablespoons KIKKOMAN® Stir-Fry Sauce
1 teaspoon cornstarch
2 large cloves garlic, minced
2 tablespoons vegetable oil, divided
1 medium onion, cut into ¾-inch chunks
2 large carrots, cut into julienne strips
1 pound fresh spinach, washed and drained
½ pound fresh mushrooms, sliced
⅓ cup KIKKOMAN® Stir-Fry Sauce

Prepare Fiery Walnuts. Cut beef across grain into thin slices, then into narrow strips. Combine 2 tablespoons stir-fry sauce, cornstarch and garlic in medium bowl; stir in beef. Heat 1 tablespoon oil in hot wok or large skillet over medium-high heat. Add beef and stir-fry 1½ minutes; remove. Heat remaining 1 tablespoon oil in same pan. Add onion; stir-fry 2 minutes. Add carrots; stir-fry 1 minute. Add spinach and mushrooms; stir-fry 2 minutes, or until spinach is wilted. Add beef and ⅓ cup stir-fry sauce; cook and stir only until beef and vegetables are coated with sauce and heated through. Remove from heat; stir in Fiery Walnuts and serve immediately.

Makes 6 servings

Fiery Walnuts: Combine 2 teaspoons vegetable oil, ¼ teaspoon ground red pepper (cayenne) and ⅛ teaspoon salt in small skillet; heat over medium heat until hot. Add ¾ cup walnut halves or large pieces. Cook, stirring, 1 minute, or until walnuts are coated. Turn out onto small baking sheet; spread out in single layer. Bake in 350°F oven 7 minutes, or until golden. Cool.

Pork Loin Roasted in Chili-Spice Sauce

1 cup chopped onion
¼ cup orange juice
2 cloves garlic
1 tablespoon cider vinegar
1½ teaspoons chili powder
¼ teaspoon dried thyme leaves
¼ teaspoon ground cumin
¼ teaspoon ground cinnamon
⅛ teaspoon ground allspice
⅛ teaspoon ground cloves
1½ pounds pork loin, fat trimmed
3 firm large bananas
2 limes
1 ripe large papaya, peeled, seeded and cubed
1 green onion, minced

Preheat oven to 350°F. Combine onion, orange juice and garlic in food processor; process until finely chopped. Pour into medium saucepan; stir in vinegar, chili powder, thyme, cumin, cinnamon, allspice and cloves. Simmer over medium-high heat about 5 minutes or until thickened. Cut ¼-inch-deep lengthwise slits down top and bottom of roast at 1½-inch intervals. Spread about 1 tablespoon spice paste over bottom; place roast in baking pan. Spread remaining 2 tablespoons spice paste over sides and top, working mixture into slits. Cover. Bake 45 minutes or until meat thermometer registers 140°F.

Remove roast from oven; increase oven temperature to 450°F. Pour off liquid; discard. Return roast to oven and bake, uncovered, 15 minutes or until spice mixture browns lightly and meat thermometer registers 150°F in center of roast. Remove from oven; tent with foil and let stand 5 minutes before slicing.

Meanwhile, spray 9-inch pie plate or cake pan with nonstick cooking spray. Peel bananas and slice diagonally into ½-inch-thick pieces. Place in pan. Squeeze juice from 1 lime over bananas; toss to coat evenly. Cover; bake in oven while roast stands or until hot. Stir in papaya, juice of remaining lime and green onion. Serve with roast. *Makes 6 servings*

Greek Pork Stew

¼ cup olive oil
1 pork tenderloin, cut into ½-inch cubes (about 2½ pounds)
½ pound small white onions, cut into halves
3 cloves garlic, chopped
1¼ cups dry red wine
1 can (6 ounces) tomato paste
1 can (14½ ounces) ready-to-serve beef broth
2 tablespoons balsamic vinegar or red wine vinegar
2 bay leaves
1½ teaspoons ground cinnamon
⅛ teaspoon ground coriander
   Hot cooked rice (optional)

Heat oil in 5-quart Dutch oven over medium-high heat. Brown half of pork in Dutch oven. Remove with slotted spoon; set aside. Brown remaining pork. Remove with slotted spoon; set aside.

Add onions and garlic to Dutch oven. Cook and stir about 5 minutes or until onion is soft. Return pork to Dutch oven.

Combine wine and tomato paste in small bowl until blended; add to pork. Stir in broth, vinegar, bay leaves, cinnamon and coriander. Bring to a boil over high heat. Reduce heat to low. Cover and simmer 45 minutes or until pork is fork-tender. Remove bay leaves before serving. Serve with rice. *Makes 6 to 8 servings*

Stuffed Salisbury Steak with Mushroom & Onion Topping

2 pounds ground beef
¼ cup FRENCH'S® Worcestershire Sauce
2⅔ cups FRENCH'S® French Fried Onions, divided
1 teaspoon garlic salt
½ teaspoon ground black pepper
4 ounces Cheddar cheese, cut into 6 sticks (about 2×½×½ inches)
   Mushroom Topping (recipe follows)

Combine beef, Worcestershire, *1⅓ cups* French Fried Onions, garlic salt and pepper. Divide meat evenly into 6 portions. Place 1 stick cheese in center of each portion, firmly pressing and shaping meat into ovals around cheese.

Place steaks on grid. Grill over medium-high coals 15 minutes or until meat thermometer inserted into beef reaches 160°F, turning once. Serve with Mushroom Topping and sprinkle with remaining *1⅓ cups* onions. *Makes 6 servings*

Mushroom Topping

2 tablespoons butter or margarine
1 package (12 ounces) mushrooms, wiped clean and quartered
2 tablespoons FRENCH'S® Worcestershire Sauce

Melt butter in large skillet over medium-high heat. Add mushrooms; cook 5 minutes or until browned, stirring often. Add Worcestershire. Reduce heat to low. Cook 5 minutes, stirring occasionally. *Makes 6 servings*

Prep Time: 25 minutes

Cook Time: 25 minutes

Swedish Meatballs

1½ cups fresh bread crumbs
1 cup heavy cream
2 tablespoons butter or margarine,
    divided
1 small onion, chopped
1 pound ground beef
½ pound ground pork
3 tablespoons chopped fresh parsley,
    divided
1½ teaspoons salt
¼ teaspoon black pepper
¼ teaspoon ground allspice
1 cup beef broth
1 cup sour cream
1 tablespoon all-purpose flour

Combine bread crumbs and cream in small bowl; mix well. Let stand 10 minutes. Melt 1 tablespoon butter in large skillet over medium heat. Add onion. Cook and stir 5 minutes or until onion is tender. Combine beef, pork, bread crumb mixture, onion, 2 tablespoons parsley, salt, pepper and allspice in large bowl; mix well. Cover; refrigerate 1 hour.

Shape meat mixture into 1-inch-thick square on cutting board. Cut into 36 squares. Shape each square into a ball. Melt remaining 1 tablespoon butter in same large skillet over medium heat. Add meatballs. Cook 10 minutes or until browned on all sides and no longer pink in center. Remove meatballs from skillet; drain on paper towels.

Drain drippings from skillet; discard. Pour broth into skillet. Heat over medium-high heat, stirring frequently and scraping up any browned bits. Reduce heat to low.

Combine sour cream and flour; mix well. Stir sour cream mixture into skillet. Cook 5 minutes, stirring constantly. Do not boil. Add meatballs. Cook 5 minutes more. Sprinkle with remaining 1 tablespoon parsley. Garnish as desired.

Makes 5 to 6 servings

Ham, Pepper & Onion Pizza with Two Cheeses

1 package pizza dough mix *or*
    1 prepared (14-inch) pizza crust
3 cloves garlic, minced
½ cup extra-virgin olive oil, divided
2 cups chopped plum tomatoes
1½ cups prepared barbecue sauce
¼ cup dried oregano leaves
3 cups (12 ounces) shredded
    mozzarella cheese
1 cup freshly grated Parmesan
    cheese
2 pounds HILLSHIRE FARM® Ham, cut
    into strips
1 red onion, thinly sliced
1 green bell pepper, thinly sliced
1 tablespoon pine nuts (optional)

Preheat oven to 425°F. Prepare pizza dough according to package directions; spread dough onto 14-inch round baking sheet. (If using prepared crust, place crust on baking sheet.)

Sauté garlic in ¼ cup oil 5 minutes in medium saucepan over medium heat. Add tomatoes, barbecue sauce and oregano. Bring to a gentle boil; reduce heat to medium. Simmer 20 to 30 minutes or until sauce is thickened.

Brush pizza dough with 2 tablespoons oil. Cover dough with cheeses, leaving ½-inch border around edge. Cover cheese with barbecue sauce mixture; arrange Ham, onion and pepper over sauce. Drizzle pizza with remaining 2 tablespoons oil; sprinkle with pine nuts, if desired. Bake 20 minutes. Slice and serve.

Makes 4 servings

Swedish Meatballs

Thai Pork Burritos

1 pound lean ground pork
2 tablespoons grated fresh ginger
　　root
1 garlic clove, peeled and crushed
2 cups coleslaw mix with carrots
1 small onion, thinly sliced
3 tablespoons soy sauce
2 tablespoons lime juice
1 tablespoon honey
2 teaspoons ground coriander
1 teaspoon sesame oil
½ teaspoon crushed red pepper
4 large (10-inch) flour tortillas,
　　warmed
　　Fresh cilantro, chopped (optional)

Heat large nonstick skillet over high heat. Add pork; cook and stir until pork is no longer pink, 3 to 4 minutes. Stir in ginger and garlic. Add coleslaw mix and onion and stir-fry with pork for 2 minutes, until vegetables are wilted. Combine all remaining ingredients except tortillas and cilantro in small bowl and add to skillet. Stir constantly to blend well, about 1 minute. Spoon equal portions of mixture onto warm flour tortillas and garnish with cilantro, if desired. Roll up to enclose filling and serve. *Makes 4 servings*

Prep Time: 15 minutes

Favorite recipe from **National Pork Producers Council**

Onion & Pepper Cheesesteaks

2 medium onions, thinly sliced
1 cup red, yellow and/or green bell
　　pepper strips
2 tablespoons PARKAY® 70%
　　Vegetable Oil Spread
½ cup GREY POUPON® Dijon
　　Mustard, divided
1 tablespoon honey
4 (6- to 8-inch) steak rolls
8 frozen sandwich steaks, cooked
1 cup shredded Cheddar cheese
　　(4 ounces)

In large skillet, over medium-high heat, sauté onions and bell pepper in spread until tender. Stir in 6 tablespoons mustard and honey; reduce heat and cook 2 minutes. Keep warm.

Cut rolls in half lengthwise, not cutting completely through rolls; brush cut sides of rolls with remaining mustard. Broil rolls, cut-sides up, until golden. Top each roll with cooked steaks, onion mixture and cheese. Broil for 1 minute more or until cheese melts. Close sandwiches and serve immediately. *Makes 4 servings*

Onion & Pepper Cheesesteak

Sausage, Peppers & Onions with Grilled Polenta

5 cups canned chicken broth
1½ cups Italian polenta or yellow cornmeal
1½ cups cooked fresh corn or thawed frozen corn
2 tablespoons butter or margarine
1 cup (4 ounces) freshly grated Parmesan cheese
6 Italian-style sausages
2 small to medium red onions, sliced into rounds
1 each medium red and green bell pepper, cored, seeded and cut into 1-inch-wide strips
½ cup Marsala or sweet vermouth (optional)
Olive oil

To make polenta, bring chicken broth to a boil in large pot. Add polenta and cook at a gentle boil, stirring frequently, about 30 minutes. If polenta starts to stick and burn bottom of pot, add up to ½ cup water. During last 5 minutes of cooking, stir in corn and butter. Remove from heat; stir in Parmesan cheese. Transfer polenta into greased 13×9-inch baking pan; let cool until firm and set enough to cut. (Polenta can be prepared a day ahead and held in refrigerator.)

Prick each sausage in 4 or 5 places with fork. Place sausages, red onions and bell peppers in large shallow glass dish or large heavy plastic food storage bag. Pour Marsala over food; cover dish or close bag. Marinate in refrigerator up to 4 hours, turning sausages and vegetables several times. (If you don't wish to marinate sausages and vegetables in Marsala, just eliminate this step.)

Oil hot grid to help prevent sticking. Cut polenta into squares, then cut into triangles, if desired. Brush one side with oil. Grill polenta oil side down, on a covered grill, over medium **KINGSFORD®** Briquets, about 4 minutes until lightly toasted. Halfway through cooking time, brush top with oil, then turn and continue grilling. Move polenta to edge of grill to keep warm.

When coals are medium-low, drain sausages and vegetables from wine; discard wine. Grill sausages on covered grill, 15 to 20 minutes until cooked through, turning several times. After sausages have cooked 10 minutes, place vegetables in center of grid. Grill vegetables 10 to 12 minutes until tender, turning once or twice.

Makes 6 servings

Polska Kielbasa Simmered in Beer and Onions

4 tablespoons butter
4 onions, thinly sliced
1 pound HILLSHIRE FARM® Polska Kielbasa, diagonally sliced into ¼-inch pieces
1 bottle (12 ounces) beer

Melt butter in large skillet over medium heat; sauté onions 4 to 5 minutes. Add Polska Kielbasa; brown 3 to 4 minutes on each side. Pour beer into skillet; bring to a boil. Reduce heat and simmer, uncovered, 25 minutes. *Makes 4 to 6 servings*

Sausage, Peppers & Onions with Grilled Polenta

Poultry Perfection

Creole Chicken

1½ tablespoons vegetable oil
1 whole chicken, cut up, or 2 pounds chicken pieces
1½ tablespoons butter or margarine
1 medium onion, thinly sliced
2 teaspoons LAWRY'S® Garlic Powder with Parsley
1½ teaspoons LAWRY'S® Seasoned Salt
1 teaspoon LAWRY'S® Seasoned Pepper
1 can (8 ounces) tomato sauce
½ cup red wine
3 medium tomatoes, chopped
1 red bell pepper, sliced into strips
1 green bell pepper, sliced into strips
3 cups hot cooked rice

In large skillet, heat oil. Cook chicken over medium high heat until brown, about 5 minutes. Remove and set aside. In same skillet, melt butter; cook onion over medium high heat until tender. Add Garlic Powder with Parsley, Seasoned Salt and Seasoned Pepper. Return chicken pieces to skillet. Add remaining ingredients except rice. Cover and simmer over low heat 30 to 40 minutes until chicken is cooked. Serve over rice.   *Makes 4 to 6 servings*

Turkey with Mustard Sauce

1 tablespoon butter or margarine
1 pound turkey cutlets
1 cup BIRDS EYE® frozen Mixed Vegetables
1 box (10 ounces) BIRDS EYE® frozen Pearl Onions in Cream Sauce
1 teaspoon spicy brown mustard

• In large nonstick skillet, melt butter over medium-high heat. Add turkey; cook until browned on both sides.

• Add mixed vegetables, onions with cream sauce and mustard; bring to boil. Reduce heat to medium-low; cover and simmer 6 to 8 minutes or until vegetables are tender and turkey is no longer pink in center.   *Makes 4 servings*

Serving Suggestion: Serve with a fresh garden salad.

Prep Time: 5 minutes

Cook Time: 15 minutes

Creole Chicken

Chicken-Asparagus Casserole

2 teaspoons vegetable oil
1 cup seeded and chopped green
    and/or red bell peppers
1 medium onion, chopped
2 cloves garlic, minced
1 can (10¾ ounces) condensed
    cream of asparagus soup
2 eggs
1 container (8 ounces) ricotta cheese
2 cups (8 ounces) shredded Cheddar
    cheese, divided
1½ cups chopped cooked chicken
1 package (10 ounces) frozen
    chopped asparagus,* thawed and
    drained
8 ounces egg noodles, cooked
    Ground black pepper (optional)

*Or, substitute ½ pound fresh asparagus cut into
½-inch pieces. Bring 6 cups water to a boil over high
heat in large saucepan. Add fresh asparagus. Reduce
heat to medium. Cover and cook 5 to 8 minutes or
until crisp-tender. Drain.

1. Preheat oven to 350°F. Grease 13×9-
inch casserole; set aside.

2. Heat oil in small skillet over medium
heat. Add bell peppers, onion and garlic;
cook and stir until crisp-tender.

3. Mix soup, eggs, ricotta cheese and
1 cup Cheddar cheese in large bowl until
well blended. Add onion mixture, chicken,
asparagus and noodles; mix well. Season
with pepper, if desired.

4. Spread mixture evenly in prepared
casserole. Top with remaining 1 cup
Cheddar cheese.

5. Bake 30 minutes or until center is set
and cheese is bubbly. Let stand 5 minutes
before serving. Garnish as desired.

Makes 12 servings

Broiled Chicken with Honeyed Onion Sauce

2 pounds boneless skinless chicken
    thighs
4 teaspoons olive oil, divided
1 teaspoon paprika
1 teaspoon dried oregano leaves
1 teaspoon salt, divided
½ teaspoon ground cumin
¼ teaspoon black pepper
1 onion, sliced
2 cloves garlic, minced
¼ cup golden raisins
¼ cup honey
2 tablespoons lemon juice

1. Preheat broiler. Rub chicken with
2 teaspoons olive oil. Combine paprika,
oregano, ½ teaspoon salt, cumin and
pepper; rub mixture over chicken.

2. Place chicken on broiler pan. Broil about
6 inches from heat 5 minutes per side or
until chicken is no longer pink in center.

3. While chicken is cooking, heat
remaining 2 teaspoons oil in medium
nonstick skillet. Add onion and garlic; cook
about 8 minutes or until onion is dark
golden brown, stirring occasionally.

4. Stir in raisins, honey, lemon juice,
remaining ½ teaspoon salt and ¼ cup
water. Simmer, uncovered, until slightly
thickened. Spoon sauce over chicken.

Makes 4 servings

Serving Suggestion: Serve with a quick-
cooking rice pilaf and mixed green salad.

Prep and Cook Time: 28 minutes

Chicken-Asparagus Casserole

Chicken Cacciatore

1 tablespoon olive oil
1 broiler-fryer chicken (3 to 3½ pounds), cut into 8 pieces
4 ounces fresh mushrooms, finely chopped
1 medium onion, chopped
1 clove garlic, minced
½ cup dry white wine
1 tablespoon plus 1½ teaspoons white wine vinegar
½ cup chicken broth
1 teaspoon dried basil leaves, crushed
½ teaspoon dried marjoram leaves, crushed
½ teaspoon salt
⅛ teaspoon pepper
1 can (14½ ounces) whole tomatoes, undrained
8 Italian- or Greek-style black olives, halved, pitted
1 tablespoon chopped fresh parsley
Hot cooked pasta
Fresh marjoram leaves for garnish

Heat oil in large skillet over medium heat. Add as many chicken pieces in single layer without crowding to hot oil. Cook 8 minutes per side or until chicken is brown; remove chicken with slotted spatula to Dutch oven. Repeat with remaining chicken pieces.

Add mushrooms and onion to drippings remaining in skillet. Cook and stir over medium heat 5 minutes or until onion is soft. Add garlic; cook and stir 30 seconds. Add wine and vinegar; cook over medium-high heat 5 minutes or until liquid is almost evaporated. Stir in broth, basil, marjoram, salt and pepper. Remove from heat.

Press tomatoes and juice through sieve into onion mixture; discard seeds. Bring to a boil over medium-high heat; boil, uncovered, 2 minutes. Pour tomato-onion mixture over chicken. Bring to a boil; reduce heat to low. Cover and simmer 25 minutes or until chicken is tender and juices run clear when pierced with fork. Remove chicken with slotted spatula to heated serving dish; keep warm.

Bring tomato-onion sauce to a boil over medium-high heat; boil, uncovered, 5 minutes. Add olives and parsley to sauce; cook 1 minute more. Pour sauce over chicken and pasta. Garnish, if desired.

Makes 4 to 6 servings

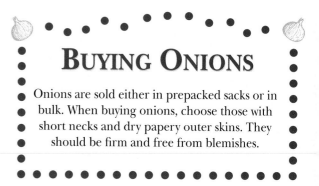

Buying Onions

Onions are sold either in prepacked sacks or in bulk. When buying onions, choose those with short necks and dry papery outer skins. They should be firm and free from blemishes.

Chicken Cacciatore

Baked Chicken and Garlic Orzo

Nonstick cooking spray
4 chicken breast halves, skinned
¼ cup dry white wine
10 ounces uncooked orzo pasta
1 cup chopped onion
4 cloves garlic, minced
2 tablespoons chopped fresh parsley
1 teaspoon dried oregano leaves
1 can (about 14 ounces) fat-free reduced-sodium chicken broth
¼ cup water
Paprika
1 teaspoon lemon pepper
¼ teaspoon salt
2 teaspoons olive oil
1 lemon, cut into 8 wedges

1. Preheat oven to 350°F. Spray large nonstick skillet with cooking spray. Heat over high heat until hot. Add chicken breast halves. Cook, meat side down, 1 to 2 minutes or until lightly browned; set aside.

2. Reduce heat to medium-high; add wine. Stir with flat spatula, scraping brown bits from bottom of pan. Cook 30 seconds or until slightly reduced; set aside.

3. Spray 9-inch square baking pan with nonstick cooking spray. Add pasta, onion, garlic, parsley, oregano, chicken broth, water and wine mixture; stir. Place chicken breasts on top. Sprinkle lightly with paprika and lemon pepper. Bake, uncovered, 1 hour and 10 minutes. Remove chicken. Add salt and olive oil to baking pan; mix well. Place chicken on top. Serve with fresh lemon wedges.

Makes 4 servings

Chicken Scaparella

2 slices bacon, coarsely chopped
2 tablespoons FILIPPO BERIO® Olive Oil
1 large chicken breast, split
½ cup quartered mushrooms
1 small clove garlic, minced
1 cup plus 2 tablespoons chicken broth, divided
2 tablespoons red wine vinegar
8 small white onions, peeled
4 small new potatoes, cut into halves
½ teaspoon salt
⅛ teaspoon pepper
1 tablespoon all-purpose flour
Chopped fresh parsley

Cook bacon in skillet. Remove bacon with slotted spoon; set aside. Pour off drippings. Add oil and chicken. Brown well on all sides. Add mushrooms and garlic. Sauté several minutes, stirring occasionally. Add 1 cup broth, vinegar, onions, potatoes, salt and pepper. Cover and simmer 35 minutes until chicken and vegetables are tender.

To thicken sauce, dissolve flour in 2 tablespoons chicken broth. Stir into sauce. Cook, stirring, until thickened and smooth. Garnish with reserved bacon and parsley. *Makes 2 servings*

Chicken Scaparella

Chicken Pot Pie

1½ **pounds chicken pieces, skinned**
1 **cup chicken broth**
½ **teaspoon salt**
¼ **teaspoon black pepper**
1 **to 1½ cups reduced-fat (2%) milk**
3 **tablespoons margarine or butter**
1 **medium onion, chopped**
1 **cup sliced celery**
⅓ **cup all-purpose flour**
2 **cups frozen mixed vegetables (broccoli, carrots and cauliflower combination), thawed**
½ **teaspoon dried thyme leaves**
1 **tablespoon chopped fresh parsley** *or* 1 **teaspoon dried parsley**
1 **(9-inch) refrigerated pastry crust**
1 **egg, slightly beaten**

Combine chicken, chicken broth, salt and pepper in large saucepan over medium-high heat. Bring to a boil. Reduce heat to low. Cover; simmer 30 minutes or until juices run clear.

Remove chicken and let cool. Pour remaining chicken broth mixture into glass measure. Let stand; spoon off fat. Add enough milk to broth mixture to equal 2½ cups. Remove chicken from bones and cut into ½-inch pieces.

Melt margarine in same saucepan over medium heat. Add onion and celery. Cook and stir 3 minutes. Stir in flour until well blended. Gradually stir in broth mixture. Cook, stirring constantly, until sauce thickens and boils. Add chicken, vegetables, thyme and parsley. Pour into 1½-quart deep casserole.

Preheat oven to 400°F. Roll out pastry 1 inch larger than diameter of casserole on lightly floured surface. Cut slits in pastry for venting air. Place pastry on top of casserole. Roll edges and cut away extra pastry; flute edges. Reroll scraps to cut into decorative designs. Place on top of pastry. Brush pastry with beaten egg. Bake about 30 minutes until crust is golden brown and filling is bubbling.

Makes about 6 cups or 4 servings

Southwest Turkey Tenderloin Stew

1 **package (about 1½ pounds) turkey tenderloins, cut into ¾-inch pieces**
1 **tablespoon chili powder**
1 **teaspoon ground cumin**
¾ **teaspoon salt**
1 **red bell pepper, cut into ¾-inch pieces**
1 **green bell pepper, cut into ¾-inch pieces**
¾ **cup chopped red or yellow onion**
3 **cloves garlic, minced**
1 **can (15½ ounces) chili beans in spicy sauce, undrained**
1 **can (14½ ounces) chili-style stewed tomatoes, undrained**
¾ **cup prepared salsa or picante sauce**
Fresh cilantro (optional)

SLOW COOKER DIRECTIONS

Place turkey in slow cooker. Sprinkle chili powder, cumin and salt over turkey; toss to coat. Add red bell pepper, green bell pepper, onion, garlic, beans, tomatoes and salsa. Mix well. Cover and cook on LOW 5 hours or until turkey is no longer pink in center and vegetables are crisp-tender. Ladle into bowls. Garnish with cilantro, if desired. *Makes 6 servings*

Southwest Turkey Tenderloin Stew

Fish & Seafood

Seafood Paella

1 tablespoon olive oil
4 cloves garlic, minced
4½ cups finely chopped onions
2 cups uncooked long-grain white rice
2 cups clam juice
2 cups dry white wine
3 tablespoons fresh lemon juice
½ teaspoon paprika
¼ cup boiling water
½ teaspoon saffron or ground turmeric
1½ cups peeled and diced plum tomatoes
½ cup chopped fresh parsley
1 jar (8 ounces) roasted red peppers, drained, thinly sliced and divided
1 pound bay scallops
1½ cups frozen peas, thawed
10 clams, scrubbed
10 mussels, scrubbed
1 cup water
20 large shrimp (1 pound), shelled and deveined

Preheat oven to 375°F. Heat oil in large ovenproof skillet or paella pan over medium-low heat until hot. Add garlic and cook just until garlic sizzles. Add onions and rice; cook and stir 10 minutes or until onions are soft. Stir in clam juice, wine, lemon juice and paprika; mix well.

Combine boiling water and saffron in small bowl; stir until saffron is dissolved. Stir into onion mixture. Stir in tomatoes, parsley and half the red peppers. Bring to a boil over medium heat. Remove from heat; cover. Place on lowest shelf of oven. Bake 1 hour or until all liquid is absorbed. Remove from oven; stir in scallops and peas. Turn oven off; return paella to oven.

In Dutch oven, steam clams and mussels 4 to 6 minutes in 1 cup water, removing each as shell opens. (Discard any unopened clams or mussels.) Steam shrimp 2 to 3 minutes just until shrimp turn pink and opaque. Remove paella from oven and arrange clams, mussels and shrimp on top. Garnish with remaining red peppers. *Makes 10 servings*

Seafood Paella

Baked Fish with Potatoes and Onions

- 1 pound baking potatoes, very thinly sliced
- 1 large onion, very thinly sliced
- 1 small red or green bell pepper, thinly sliced
  Salt
  Black pepper
- ½ teaspoon dried oregano leaves, divided
- 1 pound lean fish fillets, cut 1 inch thick
- ¼ cup butter or margarine
- ¼ cup all-purpose flour
- 2 cups milk
- ¾ cup (3 ounces) shredded Cheddar cheese

Preheat oven to 375°F.

Arrange half of potatoes in buttered 3-quart casserole. Top with half of onion and half of bell pepper. Season with salt and black pepper. Sprinkle with ¼ teaspoon oregano. Arrange fish in one layer over vegetables. Arrange remaining potatoes, onion and bell pepper over fish. Season with salt, black pepper and remaining ¼ teaspoon oregano.

Melt butter in medium saucepan over medium heat. Stir in flour; cook until bubbly, stirring constantly. Gradually stir in milk. Cook until thickened, stirring constantly. Pour white sauce over casserole. Cover and bake at 40 minutes or until potatoes are tender. Sprinkle with cheese. Bake, uncovered, about 5 minutes more or until cheese is melted.

Makes 4 servings

Crystal Shrimp with Sweet & Sour Sauce

- ½ cup KIKKOMAN® Sweet & Sour Sauce
- 1 tablespoon water
- 2 teaspoons cornstarch
- ½ pound medium-size raw shrimp, peeled and deveined
- 1 egg white, beaten
- 2 tablespoons vegetable oil, divided
- 1 clove garlic, minced
- 2 carrots, cut diagonally into thin slices
- 1 medium-size green bell pepper, chunked
- 1 medium onion, chunked
- 1 tablespoon sesame seed, toasted

Blend sweet & sour sauce and water; set aside. Measure cornstarch into large plastic food storage bag. Coat shrimp with egg white; drain off excess egg. Add shrimp to cornstarch in bag; shake bag to coat shrimp. Heat 1 tablespoon oil in hot wok or large skillet over medium-high heat. Add garlic; stir-fry 10 seconds, or until fragrant. Add shrimp and stir-fry 2 minutes, or until pink; remove. Heat remaining 1 tablespoon oil in same pan over high heat. Add carrots, green pepper and onion; stir-fry 4 minutes. Add shrimp and sweet & sour sauce mixture. Cook and stir until shrimp and vegetables are coated with sauce. Remove from heat; stir in sesame seed. Serve immediately.

Makes 4 servings

Baked Fish with Potatoes and Onions

Lemon Sesame Scallops

    8 ounces whole wheat spaghetti
    3 tablespoons sesame oil, divided
    1 pound sea scallops
    ¼ cup chicken broth or clam juice
    ½ teaspoon grated lemon peel
    3 tablespoons lemon juice
    2 tablespoons oyster sauce
    1 tablespoon soy sauce
    1 tablespoon cornstarch
    1 tablespoon vegetable oil
    2 carrots, cut into julienne strips
    1 yellow bell pepper, cut into thin
        strips
    4 slices peeled fresh ginger
    1 clove garlic, minced
    6 ounces fresh snow peas, trimmed
        or 1 (6-ounce) package frozen
        snow peas, thawed
    2 green onions, thinly sliced
    1 tablespoon sesame seeds, toasted

Cook spaghetti according to package directions; drain. Place spaghetti in large bowl; toss with 2 tablespoons sesame oil. Cover to keep warm.

Rinse scallops and pat dry with paper towels; set aside. Combine broth, lemon peel, lemon juice, oyster sauce, soy sauce and cornstarch in 1-cup glass measure; set aside. Heat remaining 1 tablespoon sesame oil and vegetable oil in large skillet or wok over medium heat. Add carrots and bell pepper; stir-fry 4 to 5 minutes or until crisp-tender. Transfer to large bowl; set aside.

Add ginger and garlic to skillet. Stir-fry 1 minute over medium high-heat. Add scallops; stir-fry 1 minute. Add snow peas and onions; stir-fry 2 to 3 minutes or until peas turn bright green and scallops turn opaque. Remove slices of ginger; discard. Transfer scallop mixture to bowl with vegetable mixture, leaving any liquid in skillet.

Stir broth mixture; add to liquid in skillet. Cook and stir 5 minutes or until thickened. Return scallop mixture to skillet; cook 1 minute. Serve immediately over warm spaghetti; sprinkle with sesame seeds.

Makes 4 servings

Grilled Tuna with Salsa Salad

    1 bag (16 ounces) BIRDS EYE® frozen
        Farm Fresh Mixtures Broccoli,
        Corn & Red Peppers
    6 to 8 green onions, sliced
    1 to 2 jalapeño peppers, finely
        chopped
    1 can (14½ ounces) diced tomatoes
        with garlic and onion*
    1 tablespoon, or to taste, lime juice
        or vinegar
    4 tuna steaks, grilled as desired

*Or, substitute favorite seasoned diced tomatoes.

• In large saucepan, cook vegetables according to package directions; drain.

• In large bowl, combine vegetables, onions, peppers, tomatoes and lime juice. Let stand 15 minutes.

• Serve vegetable mixture over tuna.

Makes 4 servings

Prep Time: 5 minutes

Cook Time: 10 minutes

Lemon Sesame Scallops

Shrimp and Crab Enchiladas

1 package (1.42 ounces) LAWRY'S®
   Extra Rich & Thick Spaghetti
   Sauce Spices & Seasoning
1 can (28 ounces) whole tomatoes,
   cut up
1 can (4 ounces) diced green chiles
½ teaspoon ground cumin
1 tablespoon vegetable oil
1 onion, chopped
1 teaspoon LAWRY'S® Garlic Powder
   with Parsley
½ pound cooked medium shrimp, cut
   in half crosswise
½ pound lump crabmeat or imitation
   crab, shredded
¼ to ½ teaspoon hot pepper sauce
2 cups (8 ounces) grated Monterey
   Jack cheese, divided
6 flour tortillas

In medium saucepan, combine Extra Rich
& Thick Spaghetti Sauce Spices &
Seasonings, tomatoes, green chiles and
cumin. Bring to a boil over medium high
heat; reduce heat to low, cover and
simmer 20 minutes, stirring occasionally.
In medium skillet, heat oil. Cook onion
with Garlic Powder with Parsley over
medium high heat until onion is tender.
Remove from heat; add shrimp, crab, hot
pepper sauce and 1 cup cheese. Place
½ cup mixture on each tortilla. Roll up
securely. In 12×8×2-inch baking dish,
pour ½ cup prepared sauce. Place tortillas
seam-side down in dish. Cover with
remaining sauce. Bake in 375°F oven 15 to
20 minutes. Top with remaining 1 cup
cheese; bake an additional 15 minutes or
until cheese is melted.

Makes 6 servings

Serving Suggestion: Top with guacamole
and dairy sour cream and serve with
Mexican rice.

Blackened Snapper with Red Onion Salsa

Cajun Seasoning Mix (recipe
   follows)
Red Onion Salsa (recipe follows)
4 red snapper fillets (about 6 ounces
   each)
2 tablespoons butter

Prepare Cajun Seasoning Mix and Red
Onion Salsa; set aside. Rinse red snapper
and pat dry with paper towels. Sprinkle
with Cajun Seasoning Mix. Heat large,
heavy skillet over high heat until very hot.
Add butter and swirl skillet to coat
bottom. When butter no longer bubbles,
place fish in pan. Cook fish 6 to 8 minutes
or until surface is very brown and fish
flakes easily when tested with fork, turning
halfway through cooking. Serve with Red
Onion Salsa. *Makes 4 servings*

Cajun Seasoning Mix: Combine 2
tablespoons salt, 1 tablespoon paprika,
1½ teaspoons garlic powder, 1 teaspoon
each onion powder and ground red
pepper, ½ teaspoon ground white pepper,
½ teaspoon black pepper, ½ teaspoon
dried thyme leaves and ½ teaspoon dried
oregano leaves in small bowl. Set aside.

Red Onion Salsa

1 tablespoon vegetable oil
1 large red onion, chopped
1 clove garlic, minced
½ cup chicken broth
¼ cup dry red wine
¼ teaspoon dried thyme leaves
   Salt and black pepper to taste

Heat oil in small saucepan over medium-
high heat. Add onion; cover and cook
5 minutes. Add garlic; cook 1 minute. Add
remaining ingredients; cover and cook 10
minutes. Uncover; cook until liquid
reduces to ¼ cup.

Brazilian Corn and Shrimp Moqueca Casserole

2 tablespoons olive oil
½ cup chopped onion
¼ cup chopped green bell pepper
¼ cup tomato sauce
2 tablespoons chopped parsley
½ teaspoon TABASCO® brand Pepper
  Sauce
1 pound medium cooked shrimp
  Salt to taste
2 tablespoons all-purpose flour
1 cup milk
1 can (16 ounces) cream-style corn
  Grated Parmesan cheese

In large oven-proof skillet over medium-high heat, heat oil. Add onion, bell pepper, tomato sauce, parsley and TABASCO® Sauce and cook, stirring occasionally, for 5 minutes. Add shrimp and salt. Cover and reduce heat to low, and simmer for 2 to 3 minutes. Preheat oven to 375°F. Sprinkle flour over shrimp mixture; stir. Add milk gradually, stirring after each addition. Cook over medium heat until mixture thickens. Remove from heat. Pour corn over mixture; do not stir. Sprinkle with Parmesan cheese. Bake for 30 minutes or until browned.

Makes 4 servings

Grilled Salmon Fillets, Asparagus and Onions

½ teaspoon paprika, preferably sweet
  Hungarian
6 salmon fillets (6 to 8 ounces *each*)
⅓ cup bottled honey-Dijon marinade
  or barbecue sauce
1 bunch (about 1 pound) fresh
  asparagus spears, ends trimmed
1 large red or sweet onion, cut into
  ¼-inch slices
1 tablespoon olive oil

1. Prepare grill for grilling. Sprinkle paprika evenly over salmon fillets. Brush marinade over salmon; let stand at room temperature 15 minutes.

2. Brush asparagus and onion slices with olive oil; season with salt and pepper.

3. Place salmon, skin side down, in center of grid over medium coals. Arrange asparagus spears and onion slices around salmon on grid. Grill salmon and vegetables over covered grill 5 minutes. Turn asparagus and onion slices. Grill 5 to 6 minutes more or until salmon flakes easily when tested with a fork and vegetables are crisp-tender. Separate onion slices into rings; arrange over asparagus.   *Makes 6 servings*

Prep and Cook Time: 26 minutes

Pasta with Shrimp, Broccoli and Red Pepper

8 ounces uncooked capellini, linguine or thin spaghetti
2 tablespoons FILIPPO BERIO® Olive Oil
1 medium onion, finely chopped
1 clove garlic, minced
1 bunch fresh broccoli, trimmed and separated into florets
½ cup chicken broth
8 ounces cooked peeled and deveined shrimp
1 red bell pepper, seeded and thinly sliced
2 tablespoons chopped fresh Italian parsley
1 fresh jalapeño pepper, seeded and minced
Salt and freshly ground black pepper

Cook pasta according to package directions until al dente (tender but still firm). Drain. Meanwhile, in large saucepan or Dutch oven, heat olive oil over medium heat until hot. Add onion and garlic; cook and stir 5 minutes or until onion is tender. Add broccoli and broth. Cover; reduce heat to low. Simmer 8 to 10 minutes or until broccoli is tender-crisp. Add shrimp, bell pepper, parsley and jalapeño pepper; stir occasionally until heated through. Add pasta to broccoli mixture; toss until lightly coated. Season to taste with salt and black pepper. *Makes 4 servings*

Lemon-Garlic Shrimp

1 package (6.2 ounces) RICE-A-RONI® With ⅓ Less Salt Broccoli Au Gratin
1 tablespoon margarine or butter
1 pound raw medium shrimp, shelled and deveined or large scallops, cut into halves
1 medium red or green bell pepper, cut into short thin strips
2 cloves garlic, minced
½ teaspoon Italian seasoning
½ cup reduced-sodium or regular chicken broth
1 tablespoon lemon juice
1 tablespoon cornstarch
3 medium green onions, cut into ½-inch pieces
1 teaspoon grated lemon peel

1. Prepare Rice-A-Roni® Mix as package directs.

2. While Rice-A-Roni® is simmering, heat margarine in second large skillet or wok over medium-high heat. Add shrimp, red pepper, garlic and Italian seasoning. Stir-fry 3 to 4 minutes or until shrimp is opaque.

3. Combine chicken broth, lemon juice and cornstarch, mixing until smooth. Add broth mixture and onions to skillet. Stir-fry 2 to 3 minutes or until sauce thickens.

4. Stir ½ teaspoon lemon peel into rice. Serve rice topped with shrimp mixture; sprinkle with remaining ½ teaspoon lemon peel. *Makes 4 servings*

Lemon-Garlic Shrimp

Seafood Stew

2 tablespoons butter or margarine
1 cup chopped onion
1 cup green bell pepper strips
1 teaspoon dried dill weed
   Dash ground red pepper
1 can (14½ ounces) diced tomatoes,
   undrained
½ cup white wine
2 tablespoons lime juice
8 ounces swordfish steak, cut into
   1-inch cubes
8 ounces bay or sea scallops, cut into
   quarters
1 bottle (8 ounces) clam juice
2 tablespoons cornstarch
2 cups frozen diced potatoes,
   thawed and drained
8 ounces frozen cooked medium
   shrimp, thawed and drained
½ cup whipping cream

1. Melt butter in Dutch oven over medium-high heat. Add onion, bell pepper, dill weed and red pepper; cook and stir 5 minutes or until vegetables are tender.

2. Reduce heat to medium. Add tomatoes with juice, wine and lime juice; bring to a boil. Add swordfish and scallops; cook and stir 2 minutes.

3. Combine clam juice and cornstarch in small bowl; stir until smooth.

4. Increase heat to high. Add potatoes, shrimp, whipping cream and clam juice mixture; bring to a boil. Season to taste with salt and black pepper.

Makes 6 servings

Serving Suggestion: For a special touch, garnish stew with fresh lemon wedges and basil leaves.

Prep and Cook Time: 20 minutes

Easy Tuna & Pasta Pot Pie

1 tablespoon margarine or butter
1 large onion, chopped
1½ cups cooked small shell pasta or
   elbow macaroni
1 can (10¾ ounces) condensed
   cream of celery or mushroom
   soup, undiluted
1 cup frozen peas, thawed
1 can (6 ounces) tuna in water,
   drained and broken into pieces
½ cup sour cream
½ teaspoon dried dill weed
¼ teaspoon salt
1 package (7.5 ounces) refrigerated
   buttermilk or country biscuits

1. Preheat oven to 400°F. Melt margarine in medium ovenproof skillet over medium heat. Add onion; cook 5 minutes, stirring occasionally.

2. Stir in pasta, soup, peas, tuna, sour cream, dill and salt; mix well. Cook 3 minutes or until hot. Press mixture down in skillet to form even layer.

3. Unwrap biscuit dough; arrange individual biscuits over tuna mixture. Bake 15 minutes or until biscuits are golden brown and tuna mixture is bubbly.

Makes 5 servings

Prep and Cook Time: 28 minutes

Easy Tuna & Pasta Pot Pie

Soups & Salads

Oniony Mushroom Soup

   2 cans (10¾ ounces each) condensed
       golden mushroom soup
   1 can (13¾ ounces) reduced-sodium
       beef broth
   1⅓ cups FRENCH'S® French Fried
       Onions, divided
   ½ cup water
   ⅓ cup dry sherry wine
   4 slices French bread, cut ½ inch
       thick
   1 tablespoon olive oil
   1 clove garlic, finely minced
   1 cup (4 ounces) shredded Swiss
       cheese

Combine mushroom soup, beef broth,
1 cup French Fried Onions, water and
sherry in large saucepan. Bring to a boil
over medium-high heat, stirring often.
Reduce heat to low. Simmer 15 minutes,
stirring occasionally.

Preheat broiler. Place bread on baking
sheet. Combine oil and garlic; brush over
both sides of bread. Broil until toasted and
crisp, turning once.

Ladle soup into 4 broiler-safe bowls. Place
1 slice of bread in each bowl. Sprinkle
evenly with cheese and remaining *⅓ cup*
onions. Place bowls on baking sheet. Place
under broiler about 1 minute or until
cheese is melted and onions are golden.

Makes 4 servings

Greek Pasta Salad

   ½ pound extra-lean (90% lean)
       ground beef
   ⅓ cup chopped fresh mint *or*
       2 tablespoons dried mint leaves
   1 clove garlic, minced
   1¾ cups (about 6 ounces) small shell
       macaroni, cooked
   10 cherry tomatoes, quartered
   2 ounces feta cheese, crumbled
   ½ red bell pepper, chopped
   ½ red onion, cut into rings
   ¼ cup reduced-calorie Italian dressing
   2 tablespoons lemon juice
       Salt and freshly ground black
       pepper
       Lettuce leaves

Brown ground beef in medium skillet.
Drain. Add mint and garlic; cook
2 minutes, stirring constantly.

Spoon ground beef mixture into large
bowl. Stir in pasta, tomatoes, cheese, red
bell pepper and onion. Add dressing and
lemon juice; toss lightly. Season with salt
and black pepper to taste. Serve on
lettuce-covered salad plates.

Makes 4 servings

Note: Salad can be made up to 4 hours in
advance.

Oniony Mushroom Soup

Pasta e Fagioli

2 tablespoons olive oil
1 cup chopped onion
3 cloves garlic, minced
2 cans (14½ ounces *each*) Italian-style
  stewed tomatoes, undrained
3 cups ⅓-less-salt chicken broth
1 can (about 15 ounces) cannellini
  beans (white kidney beans),
  undrained*
¼ cup chopped fresh Italian parsley
1 teaspoon dried basil leaves
¼ teaspoon black pepper
4 ounces uncooked small shell pasta

One can (about 15 ounces) Great Northern beans, undrained, may be substituted for cannellini beans.

1. Heat oil in 4-quart Dutch oven over medium heat until hot; add onion and garlic. Cook and stir 5 minutes or until onion is tender.

2. Stir tomatoes with liquid, chicken broth, beans with liquid, parsley, basil and pepper into Dutch oven; bring to a boil over high heat, stirring occasionally. Reduce heat to low. Simmer, covered, 10 minutes.

3. Add pasta to Dutch oven. Simmer, covered, 10 to 12 minutes or until pasta is just tender. Serve immediately. Garnish as desired. *Makes 8 servings*

Classic French Onion Soup

¼ cup butter
3 large yellow onions, sliced
1 cup dry white wine
3 cans (about 14 ounces *each*) beef
  or chicken broth
½ teaspoon dried thyme
½ teaspoon salt
1 teaspoon Worcestershire sauce
1 loaf French bread, sliced and
  toasted
4 ounces shredded Swiss cheese
  Fresh thyme for garnish

SLOW COOKER DIRECTIONS

Melt butter in large skillet over high heat. Add onions, cook and stir 15 minutes or until onions are soft and lightly browned. Stir in wine.

Combine onion mixture, beef broth, thyme, salt and Worcestershire in slow cooker. Cover and cook on LOW 4 to 4½ hours. Ladle soup into 4 individual bowls; top with bread slice and cheese. Garnish with fresh thyme, if desired.
Makes 4 servings

Pasta e Fagioli

Pasta Pesto Salad

PASTA SALAD

    8 ounces three-color rotini pasta
    3 small bell peppers (green, red and
        yellow), seeded and cut into thin
        strips
    1 pint cherry tomatoes, stemmed
        and halved (2 cups)
    6 ounces (1 block) ALPINE LACE® Fat
        Free Pasteurized Process Skim
        Milk Cheese Product—For
        Mozzarella Lovers, cut into
        ½-inch cubes (1½ cups)
    1 cup thin carrot circles
    1 cup thin strips red onion
    1 cup slivered fresh basil leaves

SPICY DRESSING

    ½ cup (2 ounces) shredded ALPINE
        LACE® Fat Free Pasteurized
        Process Skim Milk Cheese
        Product—For Parmesan Lovers
    ⅓ cup firmly packed fresh parsley
    ⅓ cup extra virgin olive oil
    ⅓ cup red wine vinegar
    2 large cloves garlic
    1 tablespoon whole-grain Dijon
        mustard
    ¾ teaspoon black pepper
    ½ teaspoon salt

1. To make the Pasta Salad: Cook the pasta according to package directions until al dente. Drain in a colander, rinse under cold water and drain again. Place the pasta in a large shallow pasta bowl and toss with the remaining salad ingredients.

2 . To make the Spicy Dressing: In a food processor or blender, process all of the dressing ingredients for 30 seconds or until well blended.

3. Drizzle the dressing on the salad and toss to mix thoroughly. Cover with plastic wrap and refrigerate for 1 hour so that the flavors can blend, or let stand at room temperature for 1 hour.

Makes 6 main-dish servings

Vegetable Beef Noodle Soup

    8 ounces beef stew meat, cut into
        ½-inch pieces
    ¾ cup unpeeled cubed potato
        (1 medium)
    ½ cup sliced carrot
    1 tablespoon balsamic vinegar
    ¾ teaspoon dried thyme leaves
    ¼ teaspoon black pepper
    2½ cups fat-free reduced-sodium beef
        broth
    1 cup water
    ¼ cup prepared chili sauce or ketchup
    2 ounces uncooked thin egg noodles
    ¾ cup jarred or canned pearl onions,
        rinsed and drained
    ¼ cup frozen peas

1. Heat large saucepan over high heat until hot; add beef. Cook 3 minutes or until browned on all sides, stirring occasionally. Remove from pan.

2. Cook potato, carrot, vinegar, thyme and pepper 3 minutes in same saucepan over medium heat. Add beef broth, water and chili sauce. Bring to a boil over medium-high; add beef. Reduce heat to medium-low; simmer, covered, 30 minutes or until meat is almost fork tender.

3. Bring beef mixture to a boil over medium-high heat. Add pasta; cook, covered, 7 to 10 minutes or until pasta is tender, stirring occasionally. Add onions and peas; heat 1 minute. Serve immediately.

Makes 6 (1½-cup) servings

Pasta Pesto Salad

Oniony Bacon 'n' Egg Salad

1⅓ cups FRENCH'S® French Fried
   Onions
8 hard-cooked eggs, chopped
6 strips cooked bacon, chopped
3 plum tomatoes, seeded and
   chopped (1 cup chopped)
1 rib celery, finely chopped
½ cup low-fat mayonnaise
1 tablespoon FRENCH'S® Deli Brown
   Mustard
6 pita bread rounds, split

Place French Fried Onions in medium
microwavable bowl. Microwave on HIGH
1 minute or until golden. Combine
onions, eggs, bacon, tomatoes, celery,
mayonnaise and mustard in large bowl.
Mix just until eggs are moistened. Spoon
into pita bread rounds.

Makes 6 to 8 servings

Tip: Spoon salad into baked pastry shells
or into cooked new potato shells and serve
as an appetizer.

Prep Time: 30 minutes

Cook Time: 1 minute

Cheesy Onion Soup

2 large onions, thinly sliced
1 clove garlic, minced
¼ cup butter
2 cups tomato juice
2⅔ cups beef broth
½ cup salsa
1 cup unseasoned croutons
1 cup (4 ounces) shredded Swiss
   cheese
Additional salsa for serving

1. Cook onions, garlic and butter in
3-quart saucepan over medium-low heat
20 minutes or until onions are tender and
golden brown.

2. Stir in tomato juice, broth and ½ cup
salsa. Bring to a boil over medium-high
heat. Reduce heat to low. Simmer,
uncovered, 20 minutes.

3. Ladle soup into bowls and sprinkle with
croutons and cheese. Serve with additional
salsa.   *Makes 6 servings*

ONION TIP

Since 1982, onion consumption
has risen over 50%! Onions
provide the perfect answer to
achieving dishes that are
healthy and flavorful.

Cheesy Onion Soup

Corn and Onion Chowder

¼ pound uncooked bacon, chopped
2 medium potatoes (¾ pound), peeled and cut into ¼-inch cubes
1⅓ cups FRENCH'S® French Fried Onions, divided
½ cup chopped celery
1 tablespoon fresh thyme *or*
    ¾ teaspoon dried thyme leaves
1 bay leaf
1½ cups water
2 cans (15 ounces each) cream-style corn, undrained
1½ cups milk
½ teaspoon salt
¼ teaspoon ground white or black pepper

Cook and stir bacon in large saucepan over medium-high heat until crisp and browned. Remove with slotted spoon to paper towel. Pour off all but 1 tablespoon drippings.

Add potatoes, ⅔ *cup* French Fried Onions, celery, thyme and bay leaf to saucepan. Stir in water. Bring to a boil over medium-high heat. Reduce heat to low. Cover; simmer 10 to 12 minutes or until potatoes are fork-tender, stirring occasionally.

Stir in corn, milk, salt, pepper and reserved bacon. Cook until heated through. *Do not boil.* Discard bay leaf. Ladle into individual soup bowls. Sprinkle with remaining ⅔ *cup* onions. *Makes 6 to 8 servings*

Prep Time: 20 minutes

Cook Time: 20 minutes

Ravioli Soup

1 package (9 ounces) fresh or frozen cheese ravioli or tortellini
¾ pound hot Italian sausage, crumbled
1 can (14½ ounces) DEL MONTE® Italian Recipe Stewed Tomatoes
1 can (14 ounces) beef broth
1 can (14½ ounces) DEL MONTE® Cut Green Italian Beans, drained
2 green onions, sliced

1. Cook pasta according to package directions; drain.

2. Meanwhile, cook sausage in 5-quart pot over medium-high heat until no longer pink; drain. Add tomatoes, broth and 1¾ cups water; bring to boil.

3. Reduce heat to low; stir in pasta, green beans and green onions. Simmer until heated through. Season with pepper and sprinkle with grated Parmesan cheese, if desired. *Makes 4 servings*

Prep and Cook Time: 15 minutes

Ravioli Soup

Thai Chicken Broccoli Salad

4 ounces uncooked linguine
½ pound boneless skinless chicken breasts, cut into 2×½-inch pieces
2 cups broccoli florets
⅔ cup chopped red bell pepper
6 green onions, sliced diagonally into 1-inch pieces
¼ cup reduced-fat creamy peanut butter
2 tablespoons reduced-sodium soy sauce
2 teaspoons Oriental sesame oil
½ teaspoon red pepper flakes
⅛ teaspoon garlic powder
¼ cup unsalted peanuts, chopped

1. Cook pasta according to package directions, omitting salt. Drain.

2. Spray large nonstick skillet with nonstick cooking spray; heat over medium-high heat until hot. Add chicken; stir-fry 5 minutes or until chicken is no longer pink. Remove chicken from skillet.

3. Add broccoli and 2 tablespoons cold water to skillet. Cook, covered, 2 minutes. Uncover; cook and stir 2 minutes or until broccoli is crisp-tender. Remove broccoli from skillet. Combine pasta, chicken, broccoli, bell pepper and onions in large bowl.

4. Combine peanut butter, 2 tablespoons hot water, soy sauce, oil, red pepper and garlic powder in small bowl until well blended. Drizzle over pasta mixture; toss to coat. Top with peanuts before serving.
Makes 4 servings

Onion Soup with Pasta

3 cups sliced onions
3 cloves garlic, minced
½ teaspoon sugar
2 cans (14½ ounces *each*) reduced-sodium beef broth
½ cup uncooked small pasta stars
2 tablespoons dry sherry
¼ teaspoon salt
⅛ teaspoon black pepper
Grated Parmesan cheese

1. Spray large saucepan with nonstick cooking spray; heat over medium heat until hot. Add onions and garlic. Cook, covered, 5 to 8 minutes or until onions are wilted. Stir in sugar; cook about 15 minutes or until onion mixture is very soft and browned.

2. Add broth to saucepan; bring to a boil. Add pasta and simmer, uncovered, 6 to 8 minutes or until tender. Stir in sherry, salt and pepper. Ladle soup into bowls; sprinkle lightly with Parmesan cheese.
Makes 4 servings

Onion Soup with Pasta

Savory Sides

Oven Roasted Potatoes and Onions with Herbs

3 pounds red potatoes, cut into 1½-inch cubes
1 large sweet onion, such as Vidalia or Walla Walla, coarsely chopped
3 tablespoons olive oil
2 tablespoons butter, melted or bacon drippings
3 cloves garlic, minced
¾ teaspoon salt
¾ teaspoon coarsely ground black pepper
⅓ cup packed chopped mixed fresh herbs, such as basil, chives, parsley, oregano, rosemary, sage, tarragon and thyme

1. Preheat oven to 450°F.

2. Arrange potatoes and onion in large shallow roasting pan.

3. Combine oil, butter, garlic, salt and pepper in small bowl. Drizzle over potatoes and onion; toss well to combine.

4. Bake 30 minutes. Stir and bake 10 minutes more. Add herbs; toss well. Continue baking 10 to 15 minutes or until vegetables are tender and browned. Transfer to serving bowl. Garnish with fresh rosemary, if desired.

Makes 6 servings

Oven-Fried Tex-Mex Onion Rings

½ cup plain dry bread crumbs
⅓ cup yellow cornmeal
1½ teaspoons chili powder
⅛ to ¼ teaspoon ground red pepper
⅛ teaspoon salt
1 tablespoon plus 1½ teaspoons margarine, melted
2 medium onions (about 10 ounces), sliced ⅜ inch thick
2 egg whites

1. Preheat oven to 450°F. Spray large nonstick baking sheet with nonstick cooking spray; set aside.

2. Combine bread crumbs, cornmeal, chili powder, pepper and salt in medium shallow dish; mix well. Stir in margarine and 1 teaspoon water.

3. Separate onion slices into rings. Place egg whites in large bowl; beat lightly. Add onions; toss lightly to coat evenly. Transfer to bread crumb mixture; toss to coat evenly. Place in single layer on prepared baking sheet.

4. Bake 12 to 15 minutes or until onions are tender and coating is crisp.

Makes 6 servings

Oven Roasted Potatoes and Onions with Herbs

Original Green Bean Casserole

**1 can (10¾ ounces) condensed
    cream of mushroom soup
¾ cup milk
⅛ teaspoon ground black pepper
2 packages (9 ounces each) frozen
    cut green beans, thawed and
    drained *or* 2 cans (14.5 ounces
    each) cut green beans, drained
1⅓ cups FRENCH'S® French Fried
    Onions, divided**

Preheat oven to 350°F. Combine soup, milk and ground pepper in 1½-quart casserole; stir until well blended. Stir in beans and ⅔ cup French Fried Onions.

Bake, uncovered, 30 minutes or until hot. Stir; sprinkle with remaining ⅔ cup onions. Bake 5 minutes or until onions are golden.

Makes 6 servings

Microwave Directions: Prepare green bean mixture as above; pour into 1½-quart microwave-safe casserole. Cook, covered, on HIGH 8 to 10 minutes or until heated through. Stir beans halfway through cooking time. Top with remaining onions; cook, uncovered, 1 minute. Let stand 5 minutes.

Prep Time: 5 minutes
Cook Time: 35 minutes

Old-Fashioned Onion Rings

**½ cup buttermilk
½ cup prepared Ranch dressing
2 large onions, sliced ½-inch thick
    and separated into rings
  WESSON® Vegetable or Canola Oil
2 cups self-rising flour
2 teaspoons garlic salt
2 teaspoons lemon pepper
½ teaspoon cayenne pepper
2 eggs, slightly beaten with
    2 tablespoons water**

In a large bowl, combine buttermilk and Ranch dressing; blend well. Add onions and toss until well coated. Cover; refrigerate at least 1 hour or overnight. Fill a large deep-fry pot or electric skillet to no more than half its depth with Wesson® Oil. Heat oil between 325°F to 350°F. In a large bowl, combine flour, garlic salt, lemon pepper and cayenne pepper; blend well. Working in small batches, place onion rings in flour mixture; coat well. Remove; dip into egg mixture. Return rings to flour mixture; coat well. Lightly shake off excess flour; fry until golden brown. Drain on paper towels. Sprinkle with additional garlic salt, if desired.

Makes 4 servings

Old-Fashioned Onion Rings

Buffalo Chili Onions

½ cup FRANK'S® REDHOT® Hot Sauce
½ cup (1 stick) butter or margarine, melted or olive oil
¼ cup chili sauce
1 tablespoon chili powder
4 large sweet onions, cut into ½-inch-thick slices

Whisk together REDHOT sauce, butter, chili sauce and chili powder in medium bowl until blended; brush on onion slices.

Place onions on grid. Grill over medium-high coals 10 minutes or until tender, turning and basting often with chili mixture. Serve warm.

Makes 6 side-dish servings

Tip: Onions may be prepared ahead and grilled just before serving.

Prep Time: 10 minutes
Cook Time: 10 minutes

Country Corn Bake

2 cans (11 ounces each) Mexican-style corn, drained*
1 can (10¾ ounces) condensed cream of potato soup
½ cup milk
½ cup thinly sliced celery
1⅓ cups FRENCH'S® French Fried Onions, divided
½ cup (2 ounces) shredded Cheddar cheese
2 tablespoons bacon bits**

Or, substitute 1 bag (16 ounces) frozen kernel corn, thawed and drained.

**Or, substitute 2 slices crumbled, cooked bacon.*

Preheat oven to 375°F. Combine corn, soup, milk, celery, ⅔ cup French Fried Onions, cheese and bacon bits in large bowl. Spoon mixture into 2-quart square baking dish. Cover; bake 30 minutes or until hot and bubbly. Stir; sprinkle with remaining ⅔ cup onions. Bake, uncovered, 3 minutes or until onions are golden.
Makes 4 to 6 servings

Prep Time: 10 minutes
Cook Time: 33 minutes

Roasted Onions

2 packages (20 ounces each) frozen baby onions
4 teaspoons brown sugar
1 teaspoon LAWRY'S® Seasoned Salt
Dash LAWRY'S® Seasoned Pepper
2 tablespoons LAWRY'S® Au Jus Gravy Mix (dry mix)
½ cup water
½ cup dry white wine
3 tablespoons butter
2 tablespoons lemon juice
2 tablespoons chopped parsley (garnish)

In 2-quart baking dish, place onions and remaining ingredients except butter, lemon juice and parsley. Blend well; dot with butter. Cover and bake in 375°F oven 45 minutes; uncover and bake 15 to 20 minutes until top is glazed. Add lemon juice.
Makes 8 servings

Presentation: Sprinkle with chopped parsley before serving.

Buffalo Chili Onions

Brown Rice and Green Onion Pilaf

 2 tablespoons FILIPPO BERIO® Olive
   Oil
 ¾ cup chopped green onions, white
   part and about 2 inches of green
   part
 1 cup uncooked brown rice
 2½ cups chicken broth, defatted (see
   note) or water
 ½ teaspoon salt
   Additional green onion, green part
   sliced into matchstick-size strips
   (optional)

In heavy medium saucepan, heat olive oil over medium heat until hot. Add chopped green onions; cook and stir 3 to 4 minutes or until wilted. Add rice; cook and stir 3 to 4 minutes to coat rice with oil. Add chicken broth and salt; stir well. Bring to a boil. Cover; reduce heat to low and simmer 40 minutes or until rice is tender and liquid is absorbed. Garnish with additional green onion, if desired.

Makes 4 to 5 servings

Note: To defat chicken broth, refrigerate can of broth for at least 1 hour. Open can; use a spoon to lift out any solid fat floating on surface of broth.

Oven-Roasted Peppers and Onions

   Olive oil-flavored nonstick cooking
   spray
 2 medium green bell peppers
 2 medium red bell peppers
 2 medium yellow bell peppers
 4 small onions
 1 teaspoon Italian herb blend
 ½ teaspoon dried basil leaves
 ¼ teaspoon ground cumin

1. Preheat oven to 375°F. Spray 15×10-inch jelly-roll pan with cooking spray. Cut bell peppers into 1½-inch pieces. Cut onions into quarters. Place vegetables on prepared pan. Spray vegetables with cooking spray. Bake 20 minutes; stir. Sprinkle with herb blend, basil and cumin.

2. Increase oven temperature to 425°F. Bake 20 minutes or until edges are darkened and vegetables are crisp-tender.

Makes 6 servings

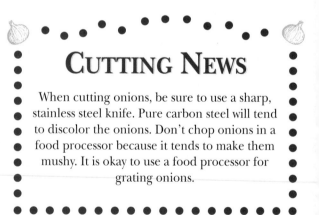

CUTTING NEWS

When cutting onions, be sure to use a sharp, stainless steel knife. Pure carbon steel will tend to discolor the onions. Don't chop onions in a food processor because it tends to make them mushy. It is okay to use a food processor for grating onions.

Oven-Roasted Peppers and Onions

Onions Baked in Their Papers

4 medium-sized yellow onions (about
2½ inches in diameter)*
1½ teaspoons mixed herbs such as
dried thyme, sage and tarragon
leaves, crushed
1 teaspoon sugar
½ teaspoon salt
Dash red pepper flakes
¼ cup butter or margarine, melted
½ cup fresh bread crumbs
Fresh tarragon sprigs, yellow
squash strips, red bell pepper
strips and chives for garnish

Choose onions with skins intact.

1. Preheat oven to 400°F. Line square baking pan with foil; set aside. Slice off stem and root ends of onions.

2. Cut 1½ X 1½-inch cone-shaped indentation in the top of each onion with paring knife. Set onions in prepared pan cut side up.

3. Stir herbs, sugar, salt and red pepper into melted butter. Add bread crumbs; mix until blended. Spoon equal amounts of crumb mixture into indentations.

4. Bake about 1 hour or until fork-tender. Garnish, if desired. Serve immediately.
Makes 4 side-dish servings

Tip: Onions make people cry because they contain an enzyme called alliinase. When this enzyme is exposed to air, it bonds with sulphur, which stimulates tear ducts. To minimize crying, chill onions before slicing or run water over them before cutting.

Creamed Pearl Onions

1 pint pearl onions (about
10 ounces)
2 tablespoons butter or margarine
2 tablespoons all-purpose flour
1 cup half-and-half
¼ teaspoon *each* salt and pepper
¼ cup dry bread crumbs
Red onion slices and fresh sage
leaves for garnish

1. To peel onions easily, blanch onions first. Cut stem end off onion; squeeze onion between thumb and forefinger to separate from its skin.

2. Place peeled onions in large saucepan with ½ inch of water; cover. Bring to a boil over high heat; reduce heat to medium-low. Simmer 15 to 20 minutes until fork-tender. Drain; set aside.

3. To make cream sauce, melt butter in small saucepan over medium heat. Blend in flour with wire whisk. Heat until mixture bubbles. Whisk in half-and-half. Cook until mixture thickens, whisking constantly. Add salt and pepper. Stir in cooked onions. Transfer creamed onions to warm serving bowl. Sprinkle with dry bread crumbs. Garnish, if desired. Serve immediately.
Makes 4 side-dish servings

Onions Baked in Their Papers

Acknowledgments

The publisher would like to thank the companies and organizations listed below for the use of their recipes in this publication.

A.1.® Steak Sauce

Birds Eye®

Del Monte Corporation

Egg Beaters® Healthy Real Egg Substitute

Filippo Berio Olive Oil

Golden Grain®

Grey Poupon® Mustard

Hillshire Farm®

Hunt-Wesson, Inc.

The HV Company

Kikkoman International Inc.

The Kingsford Products Company

Land O' Lakes, Inc.

Lawry's® Foods, Inc.

McIlhenny Company (TABASCO® Pepper Sauce)

National Onion Association

National Pork Producers Council

Reckitt & Colman Inc.

Index